COUNTRY
LIFE

This chronicle of country life, as seen through one pair of
eyes in one obscure corner of England, grew out of articles
with a similar object which I contributed to *The Spectator*.
When I began those I remembered the words addressed by
the true Peter Quince to his fellow-rustics in *A Midsummer
Night's Dream*—'This green plot shall be our stage': and
they seemed to provide an apt motto, and their author's
name no less apt a signature, for me to adopt.

I am grateful to all those readers who have shown an
interest in 'Peter Quince' and his writings, and in particular
to those who asked for a book in which these could be
expanded. This volume incorporates some material which
first appeared, in a different form, in the pages of *The
Spectator*, and my thanks are due to the editor of that journal
for the necessary permission. I must also, of course,
acknowledge my indebtedness to the shade of that estim-
able countryman whose name I took the liberty of
borrowing.

J. W. M. THOMPSON

COUNTRY LIFE

Peter Quince

with line drawings by
J. Caesar Smith

READERS UNION
Group of Book Clubs
Newton Abbot 1976

ONE

The early January days have followed a steady pattern. Each morning brought a mist which quickly faded, leaving the valley as quiet and still as an empty church. It was a prolongation of that period of calm at the heart of winter which long ago gave rise to the myth of the halcyon days. According to Pliny, a spell of tranquil weather near to the winter solstice was ordained for the particular benefit of the halcyon birds, which we know as kingfishers; they were supposed to build floating nests on the sea at this time, thus needing calm waters on which to rear their young. When they had completed this singular process, the winds were permitted to blow again and winter resumed its course. Our northern kingfishers live by more orthodox rules, but our weather obeys the old precept nonetheless, and the new year usually takes possession of a landscape that is peacefully asleep.

Even by the ancient calculation, though, the halcyon days should end as the old year dies, and this winter they have lingered beyond their proper season. The valley sank into a protracted stillness, as though life was ebbing away from the countryside, or we had somehow become trapped at the still centre of the turning year. Only the frontiers of each day, the ending of the night and then its return, caused any regular stir. The dawn brought some small signs of bustle—the odd, rattling call of a missel-thrush flying overhead or a robin singing suddenly in a hedge. At evening the world seemed briefly on the move again as the owls hooted busily in the twilight. Otherwise one could fancy that the globe had ceased to spin, that the scene was set upon a stationary, cooling planet adrift in space.

When I walked through the wood yesterday the only sound was the sigh of damp leaves beneath my feet. The ranks of beech and hornbeam stood silently, without so much as the trembling of a twig. Such an enveloping silence makes its distinctive appeal to the senses. The eye in particular responds, gaining a new awareness of detail, and I found myself noticing the pattern of moss upon the bark of a tree, or the sinister forms of a fungus which had sprouted from a fallen branch, or the convolutions of two birches which had grown together, merging their trunks high above the ground and then separating again.

When a farm dog began to bark on the other side of the valley, the effect was that of a solitary light seen from a distance at night-time; as the point of light makes the surrounding darkness more intense, so the barking of the dog accentuated the general silence. It also sounded a faint echo on the hillside, a trick I had not noticed there before, and this reminded me of the pleasure I had as a boy in discovering echo-places among the bare hills of the north country where I lived. For a moment I was transported from the damp wood to a favourite steep place which could, I remembered, repeat not merely single sounds but entire short sentences. We used to hail it in as many languages we could muster, to hear the words returned by the ghostly voice in the hillside. Later I discovered that our game had been a pastime of respectable gentlemen in the eighteenth century, with instructions published for the artificial creation of an echo in a tasteful park; the 'pleasing incident' was to be contrived by the careful siting of a barn or other building on a hill. I wonder what a modern landowner would say, if it were suggested that he might plan his buildings to provide the mild amusement of

2

listening to an echo from a thoughtfully placed seat beside a path.

As the dog fell silent, the illusion of total, blanketing stillness returned. From the hilltop I might almost have been looking down upon a map, so plain, in the cool sunlight, were the contours, the tangle of paths and lanes, and the shape of the village in the hollow. The leafless trees beside the river held their branches in the air with the immobility of an etching, the church spire pointed towards a vacant sky, and all the valley had that unguarded look which comes with sleep.

The past mingles comfortably with the present in these hours. Even the stamp put upon the landscape in Saxon times revealed itself in that clear view, and I could picture what those first settlers had found here. It had been a leafy wilderness, a land of small hills thick with oak and ash and thorn. I could imagine the pioneers arriving and clearing the level ground beside their chosen riverside site, then attacking the forest on the slopes, industriously hacking and burning to make fields for their animals and crops. The village below me looked changeless enough, yet for hundreds of years after the first huts were built it must have existed merely as a clearing in the forest. Only when the later Norman invasion had in turn sunk into history had new pioneers founded those isolated farms which I could see scattered across the slopes, and trodden those paths which skirted each patch of regained forest land.

I found it pleasant to be able to read something of this slow evolution in the landscape, which still managed to suggest a stretch of fertile land which had been gradually won from the ancient forest of England. A thousand years, or half as long again, may not be a great time in the full history of this country, but it is the span of most of what is known of the human story in this corner of it, on the fringe of East Anglia. The Romans were content merely to cut a straight road through the nearby forest, while earlier men left only faint traces behind them. There was a satisfaction in seeing the whole of that story written upon the land itself. It was a bird's-eye view of an unfinished history. I find it almost haunting that so much of the ancient England should still assert its presence within the twentieth-century mould. From the hilltop, in the halcyon calm, it was unusually clear, but all through the year I am reminded of the dead

3

generations who gradually tamed and shaped this valley. It is a landscape with figures, even though the figures are mostly unseen; and the land itself has become a palimpsest, disclosing fragments of many messages from the past. There are also unwelcome signs that this unemphatic, endearing piece of England may be passing through a halcyon period in a larger sense, a deceptive lull before irresistible forces ravage it as no winter storms have done; which may indeed be the case wherever the countryside survives today. But if so, this is at least a respite to be grateful for. The present is here to be enjoyed, the future is not to be foretold.

Meanwhile the day was dying, one more peaceful, inconspicuous death to prolong the midwinter lull. The ungrateful thought came to me, as I made my way down the hill, that the mild weather had lasted too long and was outstaying its welcome. A winter which fails to show its steel is greeted only for a time with gratitude. Afterwards, since human nature seems to rebel at an excess of tranquillity, there comes a suspicion that a necessary part of the natural order is wanting. We feel becalmed.

The man I met as I walked home evidently shared my hankering for a change. He stamped his boots irritably in the lane as he assured me that hard weather was due, and that it would unquestionably be good for all of us. Perhaps he was really thinking of his muddy fields, which need the grip of frost to tame them, or perhaps this is another point at which the puritanism in the English character comes to the surface. At any rate he sniffed the air hopefully for a promise of frost. 'I think it's turning colder,' he said in the manner of someone anxious to be first with good news. We parted to go to our firesides with encouraging promises to each other of sterner days in store, while the land sank slowly into a sea of still blackness.

This morning we had our wish: the soft, damp days came to an end at last. They did so in a dawn of mystery and strangeness, when the moisture-laden air descended upon everything in a multitude of icicles. It was not the ordinary dusting of frost, but something queer, born of an unusually abrupt plunge of the temperature. The world seemed to have grown whiskers overnight. The wire-netting round the chicken-run, the dog's bowl, the garden gate, stones and hedges, twigs and fences—all were

4

weirdly transformed by a covering of long, hairy spikes of frost. A wind from the east soon blew away the fog. The world became a still colder and harder place. The air began to sparkle, quite literally, for an infinite number of feathery diamonds were adrift in the atmosphere, each one flashing intermittently as it gyrated down. It was plain then that the know-alls who had been saying that winters had lost their sting were wrong again and that hard weather had arrived at last. This descent of minute particles of ice, each one no bigger than a speck of dust, suggests unusually cold air high above us, an atmosphere through which they fall untouched by the thaw that would merge them into snowflakes. Gilbert White observed it as a novelty at Selborne in the hard winter of 1784:

'A circumstance that I must not omit, because it was new to us, is that on Friday, December 10, being bright sunshine, the air was full of icy *spiculae*, floating in all directions, like atoms in a sunbeam let into a dark room. We thought them at first particles of the rime falling from my tall hedges; but were soon convinced to the contrary, by making our observations in open places where no rime could reach us. Were they watery particles of the air frozen as they floated, or were they evaporations from the snow frozen as they mounted?'

When I went out into the bright, frozen morning there seemed no question of any evaporation from the thin scattering of whiteness on the ground, for there was no warmth in the sun and the air had an edge which cut through my old duffle-coat. The garden was full of birds desperate for food. In the village street the old ladies scuttled into the shop with a similar urgency, scarcely pausing to commiserate with each other until the door was safely shut.

On the hill I took the upward path which, only a few hours earlier, had been soft and sticky. The footprints I had then made, and the churnings of the earth which somebody on horseback had left behind, were still there, but rock-hard in the frozen ground. There were the tracks of a rabbit and marks made by birds, all turned to stone, and the grass gave out brittle, crunching sounds as I walked. A pair of horses, trying forlornly to graze

5

an iron pasture, came up as if to complain at the harsh turn of events, although each of them, as it pushed forward for attention, moved within a visible private envelope of warm air. When I came to the edge of the wood I could hear faint, mysterious tinklings from within as the frost continued its work.

One result of the transformation was that colour seemed to have been drained from the scene, leaving only white and grey, so that from fifty yards away a spot of red at the edge of a field stood out like a beacon. It proved to be only a spent cartridge which yesterday might have passed unseen. At such times the few brightly-coloured birds which frequent the winter countryside acquire a peacock prominence. A jay launched itself from an oak-tree in a gaudy eruption of colour, a streak of pink and bright blue and gleaming white across the monochrome landscape; then a cock pheasant trailed his exotic brilliance against the grey wood. There was usually a robin near at hand as well, flaunting its patch of eye-catching plumage. A robin was the boldest of the pack of small birds which scrambled about the garden in the hope of being fed, and far out in the fields others flitted along the hedges, confidingly close as I walked along. The robin is still Chaucer's 'tame ruddock', still Donne's 'household bird, with the red stomacher'. It has forgotten most of that dread of humans which rules the lives of other birds. When I came home, I knew I should come across a robin on the path beside the churchyard, hunting for food in the thick leaf-mould beneath the lime-trees; and he might almost have been waiting for me, so closely did he follow at my heels, advancing over the ground in short, darting swoops. Perhaps it was such apparently companionable behaviour which gave rise to that recurring legend of lost travellers who perished in the wintry forest, to be piously buried beneath leaves by attendant robins. The truth, though, is that when they stay close to winter travellers in this way they are really making use of them, for in a hard frost the layers of fallen leaves are difficult for a small bird's beak to penetrate, and a man's footsteps disturb the surface sufficiently to make the food beneath accessible. That was the service I was performing on the churchyard path.

I left the robin delving in the shadows beneath the trees. As the day passed, the sky filled with cloud and the air lost some of its keenness. The sun went down, a disc of crimson in an expanse of deepening grey; and then, as the owls called across the valley, the snow began to fall, not brilliant *spiculae* now but large fleecy flakes, sailing down confidently out of the night to submerge everything beneath a billowing plain of whiteness.

TWO

The village was cut off from the outer world for one day only. That is not very long; nevertheless, even so much isolation is a quaint novelty nowadays. People cleared the snow from their paths and trudged down the centre of the village street without, for once, having to make way for motor traffic. The shop was crowded; so was the pub; most people enjoyed the sudden cessation of routine. As there was no school bus the older children had a day's uncovenanted holiday and a score of them spent it tobogganing down the steepest hillside. Their shouts and whoops sounded cheerfully across the white valley.

I doubt if country people would enjoy such isolation for long, though. It was the normal condition of life for every generation up to present times, but the circumstances which produced it and the attitude of mind which it bred have all vanished into the past. People used to live their lives on their own patch of territory, like the birds and the animals. I have an old neighbour, now nearly ninety years of age, who was thirty before he travelled farther than the local market town, five miles away, and when he went there he went on foot. I recently came across an old county guide in which the tradesmen in each village were listed, and I was impressed by the great variety of services which were available on one's doorstep in the Victorian countryside. This modest-sized village had its resident tailor and shoemaker, its thatcher and tiler, its saddler and blacksmith, its carpenter, its carrier—in addition, of course, to the butcher, baker, chandler and so on. Nowadays a superficial traveller in rural England might conclude that the only village tradesmen still flourishing were selling either frozen food to the inhabitants or antiques to tourists. That might be an exaggeration, but the abandonment of a way of life founded upon local self-sufficiency has been almost complete.

Few complain of this, but even a brief isolation by snowstorm is enough to hint at the vulnerability, as well as the breach with all previous history, inherent in our present ways. We are made to see how dependent our lives and our comforts have become upon remote forces which show no sign of caring overmuch about our welfare. And here we were, snowed in, cut off, marooned in a white wilderness.

Birds perched in the hedges with their feathers puffed out. People plodded down the lane similarly enlarged by coats and wraps and scarves. A few shovelled away enough snow to get their cars on to the road, then glowered in a fury of frustration as the wheels thrashed and slithered ineffectually, a roar of engine power producing nothing but a shivering, crabwise movement. The owners looked as helpless as fishes on a bank, stranded in an alien element.

I walked beside the river for a time. There was a semblance of a path through the snowdrifts where the arching trees had provided some shelter. At a bend in the river I caught sight of a heron, although that was not quite what I seemed to see at first: rather, a scrap of the grey sky detached itself from the mass and moved, slowly and purposefully, overhead, topping the hillside trees; and then I recognised the dignified heron outline. Something about herons—I suppose their bulk, together with their hieratic deportment—suggests that a certain respect is their due. I feel this when I come across one in the half-light of a winter evening, and see the grey, ghostlike shape rise from the water's edge and sail away, with little visible effort for so large a bird, to lose itself in a frosty sky. Often they stand impressively still in the shallow water, waiting for some prey for those fierce beaks to pounce upon or, perhaps, merely digesting what they have already swallowed: then they have a grave, religious air and I think of Dylan Thomas's 'heron-priested shore'. Once I came across a dozen herons standing in a semi-circle while another, who looked like the arch-priest, stood facing them as if conducting some important rite. I shall always remember the strangeness and seriousness of that grey group at the edge of a lake. Unhappily they saw me before I could approach closely and they lifted themselves into the air with many a sonorous and displeased croak. One day I hope to test the assertion by T. H. White that, if a heron can be stalked and surprised at close quarters, it will fall down in a kind of fit of astonishment; it sounds bizarre, but White said firmly that he had seen it happen, and he was an accomplished observer of nature. I have no great expectations of being able to get near enough to a heron to try it for myself.

Still, it was agreeable to see a heron on the wing. There must have been herons in this valley for untold centuries but they obey their own laws; and for a season recently they deserted us. I could see no apparent reason. Our little river swells into an ornamental lake in the grounds of the old rectory, and a mile or so further down it flows into some long-exhausted gravel pits which have turned into a miniature wilderness of dense vegetation and water. These are the herons' places. Nothing had changed there so far as anyone could see and yet the herons went away.

Then in their mysterious fashion they returned. One day an old man in the village said to me, 'I saw that old crane back on the water this morning,' and later I saw it for myself. But it had been years since I had heard anyone here refer to a heron as a 'crane'. There was a time, I know, when it was seldom called anything else, but the word seems almost to have passed out of use, along with most of the other vernacular names for birds, which survive chiefly in literature. I am thinking of 'throstle' for song-thrush, 'dunnock' for hedge-sparrow, 'yaffle' for green woodpecker, and the rest; there are dozens and dozens of such words, many of them peculiar to one district or region. Their tendency to fall out of use has something to do with the decay of dialects, but apart from that they belong to a time when the wild life of the countryside was a more familiar element in daily life than it is today. Nature may be studied more closely and more systematically by some people now than at any previous time, but that is not the same as the old intimacy conveyed by a whole popular vocabulary of nicknames and local words.

The fact that the village was locked inside a vast snowdrift made it, I suppose, a moment to think of these slender cobwebs of tradition which link us to our past, fragile strands like the old man remembering the word 'crane'. Very soon the snowploughs would open up the roads again and we would rejoin the twentieth century; but for a few hours we had dropped out of it all. Sometimes it is enticing to speculate about what would follow if, through some prodigious turn of history, we were to drop out of it for good. In the long view of time, after all, we have barely taken a single step away from that other, different rural order which lasted through the millennia.

And then, as daylight faded, the electricity supply failed. It was something to do with the snowstorm, we vaguely supposed, but whatever the cause the effect was unmistakable. We had slipped back even further from the familiar twentieth century. It so happened that I had to call at several houses in the village during the hours of darkness and some of the domestic scenes I came across belonged to another age: families sitting quietly in their parlours with a single candle, a couple relying upon the flickering light of a log fire, others with various sorts of oil lamp, dimly burning. One interior might have come directly from the canvas of some 'picture of the year' in the high days of the Royal Academy, with a farm labourer and his wife and their brood grouped beneath a hurricane lamp hanging from a massive oaken beam. Yet, although there was a general disposition to make remarks about returning to 'olden times', I made my way through the moonlit village thinking that one did not have to reach very far back in time to recall when this was the daily reality for many country people. My own middle-aged memory can easily summon up a countryside in which a domestic supply of electricity was a rarity. As a boy in the nineteen-thirties, I assumed as a matter of course that farms and cottages were lit by oil lamps, often of that faintly alarming variety which hissed softly to itself, giving an effect of simmering indignation; and in such houses it was usual to go to bed bearing a candlestick, which called up an escort of leaping shadows, highly stimulating to the childish imagination.

When so much changes, the fact of change ceases to register. Only a jolt like an electricity failure, or an imprisoning blizzard, reminds us of it, but there has been a far greater change in the countryman's lot over these past few years than over many centuries previously. This can make a man who has lived through most of it feel positively antediluvian, if he lets his mind dwell on the subject. It is one thing to read in Boswell that Samuel Johnson had a bald patch in the front of his wig, caused by his habit of leaning too close to the flame while reading by candlelight; but I can remember singeing my own brow in precisely that way, when reading in bed in a farmhouse by the light of one candle. To children such a recollection is a sign of almost unbelievable antiquity; but then, the countryside I knew in the nineteen-thirties does seem almost unbelievably remote. Even a motor-car, in that part of northern England which I remember, was a rarity. The horse was the source of power on the farm: and what handsome, shining, docile beasts those farm horses were in their lives of servitude. Country people used horses as their means of locomotion as well, and I can still summon up the delight for a child of bowling along a country lane in a horse-drawn trap. Human muscles were of equal importance; at harvest time the villages were deserted as every man, woman and child took to the fields. I remember the work in the hayfield continuing long after the sun had set, until the line of toiling figures faded into the dusk.

The changes in the domestic ways of the country have been no less great. Water was obtained from a pump, vegetables were supplied by one's own garden and not by a shop, cheese came from a farm, and to buy milk you either walked to the nearest farmer's kitchen door with a jug or, if lucky, had it delivered round the village by a farm man carrying a glorified bucket from which pints were ladled. The weekly wash-day was a protracted and strenuous enterprise, and some at least of the village housewives whom I can remember made their own soap, according to some inherited recipe. Cooking, including the regular baking of bread, was done almost exclusively on the kitchen range, where the fire burned for three hundred and sixty-five days each year. Bedrooms were unheated in the bitterest weather. A crust of ice formed nightly inside the windows.

No wonder the young look at me with a certain alarm if I tell them I can remember so different a world. I can even recall the day when my father pointed out a farmer marching up and down a field sowing seeds broadcast, like a Biblical figure. The nineteen-thirties are not so very distant, however, in the eye of history. Time is a deceiver. The paradox is that when we are young we believe that we ourselves have experienced all the time that is of true significance. When we have lived longer we see our own span as of no greater consequence than one beat of the heron's wing as it journeys steadily down the valley into darkness.

Times may change but time itself, in the village, is still regulated and punctuated by the church clock, which gives shape and order to each day as it passes. Until this snowbound week, I regret to say, I had accepted its regular chiming without much thought for how it came about. I like to hear it striking the hours, never more so than on a hard winter's night; the sound of midnight ringing out across the frozen scene is cheerful and companionable, sketching in the mind a community snug in their beds or sitting by the last embers of their fires, while the firm notes sound from the church tower. I had never bothered to learn precisely how this familiar signal came to be delivered with such regularity. Then I looked out at midnight upon the snowdrifts and blackness and waited to hear the twelve strokes of the bell—and nothing happened. There was a silence, except for the sound of the freezing wind in the trees.

13

It transpired that the man who unobtrusively climbs the church tower twice a week to wind the clock had influenza. There was a need for an understudy. Thus I found myself enjoying the dignity and responsibility of a temporary clock-winder, and making my way across the churchyard next evening to perform my duty. The gravestones had a surprisingly cheerful look in their coats of snow, rather like snowmen; but the air was as cold as death. Inside the church it was warmer, at least until I went through the little gothic doorway, at the foot of the tower, which leads to the spiral staircase; beyond there the stone walls were cold, the steps were cold, the imprisoned air even colder. I felt myself to be curiously isolated as I climbed up the tower. It was a longer climb than I had foreseen, and when I reached the clock chamber I seemed to have left the village far below. The wind howled like a wolf outside the thick walls and gusts came stabbing through the ventilators like lances of ice.

Not that I regretted having taken on the job for the night. Perversely, there was a kind of snugness up there in the old room surrounded by the winter night. I wondered if perhaps the crow's-nest of a sailing ship provided the same sense of slightly precarious security. Besides, the clock mechanism proved to be a noble and massive piece of nineteenth-century engineering, with huge girders of cast iron, tremendous cog wheels and finely made brass fitments gleaming in polished splendour; all looked solid and enduring, as a village timepiece should. A brass plate announced the maker's name, with his addresses in London and Derby, and also the date of its making, which indicated that we shall shortly be able to celebrate the first hundred years of our clock's service to the village. Various cables stretched out from the works at odd angles, crossing the draughty chamber on their way to the bells. They gave a touch of whimsical improvisation to the imposing construction.

To speak of 'winding' a clock is to suggest a fairly delicate, small-scale operation, but I found I had something more strenuous in hand. The winding-key was an enormous brass object, like the starting-handle for a gigantic antique motor-car; it required energetic two-handed treatment, with the handle travelling through a circle some four feet in diameter. As it revolved in my hands I could see through a hole in the floor-

14

boards that the heavy weight was slowly climbing up the tower, until it popped through the hole to hang neatly beside the handle. There was a distraction when a small, dark shape suddenly scuttled up the wall to vanish through a crack in the ceiling. I had frightened a bat out of his winter sleep. Then two other weights had to be hauled up, to sound the chimes. At the end of it I was warm enough not to notice the draughts.

Later, I heard the measured strokes of midnight with a new satisfaction. I wondered how far downwards the weights had moved since I raised them and I hoped the snow would not get in to clog the mechanism. Although time will not stop, even if all the church clocks are stilled and silenced, although 'time and the hour runs through the roughest day', still there is a fitness in marking its passage in a respectful and familiar fashion. They tell me that in up-to-date places the churches have electric clocks which do not need winding; but I think they are missing something, even when there is no failure in the electrical supply.

THREE

After starting as a sort of grand entertainment, the snow became
first humdrum, then a bore. It began to look shabby. Everyone
was relieved when at last it went away, although it left behind a
sodden scene. The sunlight glittered on the dripping trees, and
the river woke up suddenly with a roar over the sluice-gate.

This is a time when people go out to take stock of their
drenched gardens. A farmer tells me that a good blanket of snow
on the land is the best of all fertilisers; it hardly sounds the most
modern of agricultural doctrines, but I know what he means.
After snow has been on the ground there are always signs of
rapid growth to be seen. It is the iron frost and the piercing wind
which hold back the spring. When the snow is thick there are
invisible stirrings of life beneath the surface. As soon as it
departs, the season seems to have taken a long stride forward.

The grass has a new greenness, there are swelling buds on every tree and bush.

Underneath the two old apple-trees (which ought to be dispatched for having outlived their full productivity, so people tell me, although I do not believe I shall ever follow their advice) there are some patches of flecked white which suggest that bits of snow have escaped the general thaw. The unknown poet who named the flowers made one of his happier strokes when he christened the snowdrop. These are the prima donnas of the garden at this time, toughness and delicacy combined in their waxen heads and green spears. If I possessed the lordly, spacious garden which in a better-ordered universe (I tell myself) would certainly be mine, I should plant snowdrops by the thousand. It is strange that so few of the great gardens known to me have enough of them, enough to allow them to be used with the prodigality they merit, in rich drifts spreading magnificently beneath tall trees.

Usually I like to know where plants and flowers have come from, because there is a romance about the way in which men throughout history have carried them across the face of the earth; but in the case of the snowdrop it is hard to be sure. Some suggest it is a native of the damp woods of southern England, others think it an introduction from southern Europe or Asia Minor. I suppose it scarcely matters now which is the truth, since it has for so long been an indispensable part of the English winter. Botanists distinguish more than a dozen species, and the most casual of gardeners is likely to notice that what he is content to call 'snowdrops' come in a variety of different sizes and with small variations in the flowers. Again, this is not of much importance, for their principal charm in the garden depends upon mass effect.

The crocus is the ideal partner for the snowdrop in the work of cheering up this bedraggled end of winter. On days when the wind howls in the treetops, and the rain sweeps across the land like an agent of divine retribution, it is reassuring to find the blobs of bright crocus colours, deep yellow and bright purple and variously striped, springing up in the grass. But in the matter of botanical history, the crocus provides a far greater puzzle than the snowdrop. What could be stranger, or more perplexing, than that the word 'crocus' should be linked in history with the word 'crocodile'? Yet my copy of Samuel Johnson's dictionary confidently asserts that 'crocodile' means, quite simply, 'afraid of crocuses', from Greek words meaning 'saffron-fearing'; saffron being, of course, not our spring-time crocus but its relative the autumn-flowering variety. The suggestion that crocodiles should be *afraid* of crocuses seems to me as tall a story as you are likely to come across anywhere in etymology or in botany: the evidence is plain, nevertheless, that it was accepted as a fact through many centuries of scholarship. In the seventeenth century Thomas Fuller combined it with another implausible tale, to tell us that 'the crocodile's tears are never true save when he is forced where saffron groweth', and the same notion recurs in many places. Could this be, I have wondered sometimes, an early historical record of an allergy, and would a crocodile at the Zoo weep tears of terror if one threw a bunch of crocuses at him? Alas, it is hardly likely, since modern lexicographers, in their tiresomely accurate way, have put an end to the story. That it should have been accepted unquestionably for so long remains a curiosity of human credulity.

Still, I have autumn crocuses growing in my garden, should any crocodile venture in this direction. In fact, saffron grows here with rather more vigour than the kinds of crocus which are now coming into flower with such welcome effect. It, too, has long been cultivated in this country, not primarily as a flower (although it is worth its space as that alone) but as a spice and a dye of wonderful colour. Saffron-growing used to be an industry in some places, hence the name of Saffron Walden in Essex, and I read recently of an attempt to re-establish saffron as a commercial crop there. I should think it one of the most irksome crops imaginable to harvest, since the valuable part of the plant consists only of the anthers inside the flower, and they have to be picked (according to tradition) in the early hours of the morning, just as the flowers are beginning to open.

At present we dwell upon these tokens of spring in our gardens because of a general feeling that we have had our full share of winter. To be marooned by snowdrifts and blasted by winds from Siberia is enough. If the charm of our climate is its infinite variety, then let it proceed accordingly.

First, though, there was one last wintry matter to dispose of, the annual meet of the hunt on the outskirts of the village. This is not a passionate hunting community, and this quiet and well-tilled land is not outstanding hunting country. For all that, the hunt flourishes, to the mild contentment of that large majority who never themselves kill anything by way of sport. It is part of the continuing scene. It must be admitted, though, that country people today are not at all well-informed in the matter of hunting the fox. A hundred years ago, it may be, they were knowledgeable and shrewd about the business and would be equipped to discuss the points of a day's sport at length. It is not so now. There is an enthusiastic, not to say fanatical, hunting element in the community; but the rest of us do not see much of their activities except occasionally when they set out in the morning all clean and frisky, and then again when they return home weary and mud-splashed.

The local meet is a rather special case, however. Whenever the hounds come close to the village there is an immediate stir of interest. The most surprising people reveal (or claim) up-to-the-minute knowledge of the whereabouts of foxes. Conversation is salted with allusions to scent and suchlike matters; people seem to elect themselves temporary members of the hunt in imagination, and partake of the spirit of the chase. I once heard a village shopkeeper, following the hounds by bicycle, snarl 'Gerrup' at his machine as he breasted a hill, in much the tone of voice Mr Jorrocks must have used to his mutinous horse when bellowing, 'Come Hup! I say, you hugly beast!'

At the appointed hour, a piercing wind was blowing across the fields. The meeting-place was beside an old windmill at the crest of a notoriously draughty piece of rising ground, and the cold air scourged the whole landscape. As it was a weekday the turnout was not large, perhaps twenty-five people on assorted horses with about as many followers on foot or (more often) on wheels. We who were hanging about on foot passed some time telling one another that it was remarkably cold. Some of the pedestrian experts said it was an excellent day for scent, whilst others said with equal assurance that, in fact, precisely the opposite was true.

In time the cavalry moved off with a splendid clip-clopping

down the lane and began to draw a fair-sized wood, whereupon the more energetic of the village enthusiasts made their way along the edge of a ploughed field to what was thought to be a good observation point. The lazier ones went and sat inside their cars. We looked back at them with a certain disdain, until a sleety rain began to come down and the wind drove it into our faces like volleys of lilliputian arrows.

The woods echoed to the shouts and halloos of the huntsmen, the calls of the hunting horn, and the occasional outbursts of excited noise from the hounds. If you do not often witness it, it is easy to forget the sheer scale of fox-hunting; it needs great stretches of country, mile upon mile of it, and small armies of mounted men. No wonder, since space is its first requirement, that it should increasingly seem an anachronism.

The sleet came down persistently. After half an hour spent muddily scrambling along hedges and listening to the sounds of the hunt and glimpsing the hounds casting about in mounting frustration, the enthusiasm of the pedestrian followers began to grow faint. One or two thought they would go back 'and get round to the other side of the wood', which was instantly taken to mean that they were going home. Others began to make disparaging remarks about the prowess of the Master or the huntsmen, with here and there an increasingly critical estimation of the hounds' quality thrown in. The wind and the sleet together really were rather disagreeable.

It was lunch-time, for a non-hunting man at least, when the scene was all at once transformed. First the clouds cleared with a startling speed, unveiling a brilliant sun in a blue sky. The sleet ceased to plague us. Then one of the watchers sighted a fox and pointed him out to the rest. He was moving, quietly and confidently as it appeared, along the far side of the field, efficiently putting a good distance between himself and the hounds. An assortment of shouts went up from the gallery. The fox glanced across, in a manner which suggested faintly insulting indifference, and went on his way. A little later the hounds appeared in full cry, with more tremendous bellowing from the huntsmen and a great thunder of hooves as the whole gathering set off across the green turf, and the spectacle drew a shapeless cheer from the onlookers. I know that many people would have found it too rough and unrefined a spectacle to merit a cheer; others, thinking of the moments of terror and blood inseparable from it, would have recoiled in disgust from a barbarous scene. I understand such feelings, but I think the watchers by the hedge saw something else as well. There before our eyes, in the sharp winter sunlight, was the secret of what really stirs the countryman's pulse when the hounds come into his parish: the bright coats, the rollicking hounds, the headlong gallop, all in a setting of fresh green grass and leafless woods just beginning to show their spring colours, with, as it chanced, a country house of rosy brick in the middle distance. We were looking at a vestige of an England which we pine for at times in the new England of housing estates and motorways.

That was the end of it for the watchers. The hunt was swiftly out of sight and away. In the pub that evening there was a report that the fox had been killed after a spirited run. Later a contradictory rumour had it that the fox had got clean away. We will probably never know the truth unless someone makes it his particular business to find out, but judging by that fox's look of easy self-assurance I think I would put my money on him.

FOUR

There were signs of maintenance work in the rookery today: one
more hint that winter is ending. The rookery has been established in a group of elms and chestnuts for longer than anyone
can remember, and as it is only a couple of hundred yards from
my windows I see a good deal of the inhabitants' comings and
goings. They make cheerful neighbours. They never enter the
garden, to my great relief; the thought of those aggressive
foragers at work among seeds and young plants would be enough
to give a gardener a sense of panic. On the other hand they lead
such an animated communal existence, and give such exhilarating displays of aerobatics, that I almost think I should miss their
presence more than that of any other kind of bird.

I notice that they converse with each other much more than
most birds do. Throughout the breeding season, especially, the
rookery is in an almost constant state of hubbub. The voice of
the rook is remarkable, not indeed for its musicality, which is
negligible to my ears, but for its extensive range of different
sounds; it has even been said that rooks try to sing in the spring,
although I have never been able to detect any such effort. What

22

rooks do, beyond any question, is to maintain a steady outpouring of croaks and clucks and caws of astonishing variety. I wish I knew what this incessant chattering was all about. Song-birds are for the most part singing in order to demarcate and defend their territory, but there seems no territorial justification for the rook's noisy ways. Unless all this vocal activity is entirely pointless, it must represent a form of conversation. No ornithologist, so far as I am aware, has fully explained it, but there is no difficulty in picturing rooks as compulsive conversationalists, because they cling so eagerly to the company of their own kind. Many birds go about in flocks at various times of the year, but the rook lives in his own organised community through all the seasons, feeding and sleeping and playing with his tribe; and anyone who thinks it fanciful to speak of rooks 'playing' cannot have observed them very closely. At times, especially on windy days, they frolic about on the wing with the same air of boisterous enjoyment to be seen in a gang of small boys fooling about in a swimming pool. When they flock back to the rookery in the evening, they often seem to be playing about in the air for the sheer fun of it, twisting and tumbling for no conceivable reason other than urchin pleasure, like a jolly, vulgar mob at the end of a day's work.

They seem to live a mimic version of our own village life, up there in the treetops. They generally find their food out in the open farmland; in this respect, too, the rook's life in a sense resembles those of many of its human neighbours, who go out to the fields to work by day and return to the village in the evening. The rooks lead the more sociable lives, though. When I disturbed a great flock of rooks feeding in a field today I noticed that other fields nearby, all of which presumably offered much the same bill of fare to a hungry rook, were empty. If there is any practical value in this sticking together, I am not quite clear what it is; I suspect they simply like being in a crowd, as do so many human beings. When I appeared they all had to get up into the air, cawing and protesting and generally making a great fuss over the intrusion, and it seemed likely that, again as with human beings, a good communal grumble consoled them for the bother. If so, they are certainly better off in this regard than most modern farm workers.

Much of the labour of farming used to be done in companionable groups, but nowadays it is generally left to one man with a tractor. I passed such a one today and thought he might have felt a touch of envy for the milling mob of rooks nearby, if indeed he was aware of them except as a familiar, unremarked presence in the background, for he gave me a wave and a grin and looked as if he might like to break off and pass the time of day; but that sort of indulgence is not easily fitted into the strict schedules of modern agriculture. He had to stick to his work for hour upon hour. I suppose a tractor-driver has as lonely a job as anyone in the countryside, or anyone anywhere for that matter. He spends his days isolated in the smelly, noisy cabin, his eyes fixed on the ground, his body incessantly jolted as the tractor makes its droning way across the fields; he has no companion and can have little sense of contact with the world around him. Sometimes tractor-men take their dogs with them for company. The other day I saw one who had built a wooden platform beside his seat, on which his Labrador could perch when it grew bored with the endless to-ing and fro-ing.

There have always been lonely jobs on farms, of course. W. H. Hudson writes of walking across the Wiltshire downs and suddenly spotting the distant figure of a boy running across the vacant landscape. The boy, he realised, was running hard, and for a considerable distance, and was so judging his route that it would eventually bring him face to face with the solitary walker. When they finally met, Hudson inquired whether some emergency had occurred. But no: the boy, it turned out, was employed to spend his days scaring birds off the seeded fields, and his only object was to come close to another human being, for the novelty of it. 'Just to see you pass,' he said. That was in the early years of the century, yet I imagine that today's tractor-drivers, even in this more populous countryside, are no less isolated in their working hours, even though they may drive home to watch television when the evening comes. The only company my acquaintance of today had, apart from a brief glimpse of myself, was that of the flocks of rooks and gulls and lapwings who were out with him, untroubled, evidently, either by the din or by the whiff of diesel fumes which hung in the air.

The rookery is full of conscientious householders, and in this too it resembles the human community down at ground level. The rooks were pulling their huge, shapeless nests about at an early hour today, sailing across the sky with twigs gripped in their beaks, and hopping and flapping around the uppermost branches in a flurry of domestic activity and racket. It is really a rather similar state of affairs with us. The urge to spring-clean is making itself felt. Paint is in demand. The debris of winter is being cleared out of gardens. The English passion for domesticity, rural domesticity for preference, is stirring again.

I sometimes think this passion is the overflowing of a dammed stream of poetry within the race. It is in any case a passion which has left fond marks upon the villages of modern England, which with all their scars still speak eloquently of a people who love their old houses and their gardens and the haphazard comfortableness of village streets which have grown by easy stages over the centuries. If one were pessimistic, this could be seen as a last love for a dying order, and God knows there are enough forces loose in the land prepared to wipe it all out of existence before much longer; but I keep a stubborn conviction, irrational though it may be, that somehow what is so much loved will not be entirely destroyed.

Unfortunately the enemy comes not only in big battalions, with bulldozers and concrete, but also as single spies disguised as friends. I saw a couple of them in the village looking over an engaging cottage which is for sale. They had an expensive car parked nearby and they were standing by the gate discussing how they might improve the old house to suit their taste. 'We could put in a bigger window instead of that thing,' said the man, pointing to the modest lattice with its diamond panes. As I eavesdropped for a few more moments I heard mention of a 'patio', and complaints about the lowness of the ceilings, and doubts about the comfort of living under thatch.

They were drawn to the place by something, that was plain, yet if it fell into their hands the chances were that they would destroy that something without knowing what they were doing. The pattern is familiar but there remains, for me at least, a puzzle about it. People cry that they will have no more suburbia, remove themselves to a village, and instantly set to work creating their own little suburbia around them. Concrete goes down by the lorry-load, hedges give way to those hideous fences made of painted planks, and old houses which are unpretentious but altogether successful in one architectural tradition are converted into clumsy parodies of another. It is mystifying. If at the end of all their messing-about the owners had got themselves pseudo-modern houses on the cheap, then the thing would be perfectly understandable, but, of course, they pay dearly for the results. The country cottage which 'looks pretty' but lacks the full glories of suburbia is, alas, likely to be an expensive acquisition even if the buyer is content with it as it stands. If, having bought it, he then decides to transform it, he is setting out on a costly course. By the time he has said goodbye to the builders, and the plumbers, and the roofers, and the central-heating engineers, not to mention the anti-woodworm specialists, and the carpenters, and various experts such as old Joe who is the only man who knows where the drains lie, then he has probably spent enough to buy himself a couple of brand-new desirable residences with picture windows in all directions.

Country people do not despise modern houses as such: far from it. Most farm workers are happy to exchange beams and inglenooks (and damp) for a crisp new council house; but common sense is offended by this extravagant tinkering with something which is already very good of its kind, common sense and also a sense of what is decent and civilised in caring for what has been inherited from the past.

What every village needs is someone like my friend the Colonel. Since he retired he has made a devoted study of the architecture of his parish and he now possesses an affectionate knowledge, I believe, of every building within its boundaries. He is learned about cruck building, and the product of the long-defunct local brickworks, and such matters. He also seems to become aware by some instinct whenever a householder is contemplating any unfeeling assault upon the character of his property, and is swiftly on the scene in the hope of being able to represent a more respectful point of view. Since he is a man of limitless courtesy and considerable diffidence, the ensuing conversations are often lengthy and must also, I imagine, be bewildering at first to those whom he addresses. But more often than not the Colonel wins his point. He is, I feel, a great diplomatist *manqué*, since what he is in effect doing is telling a house-holder not to be an insensitive oaf, whereas the man usually ends with the feeling that he is making a brave and lonely stand against the forces of barbarism. It is a delicate transaction.

The Colonel has his defeats, of course. One that pained him acutely was when the old house standing directly across the village street from his own home suddenly appeared in a hideous new dress of blue and yellow paint. The eruption did fearful violence to the entire village scene. For once the Colonel's instinct had failed him and he had not had wind of the danger in time to influence the offender towards higher things. I dare say he was kept awake at night by the thought of the garish display outside his own windows.

After a year he steeled himself to raise the matter with the misguided man, in his customary gentle fashion. After various opaque hints, 'Don't you think', he finally brought himself to say, getting as near to a direct rebuke as was within his range, 'that perhaps it might be agreed that the—er, the *experiment* has not been a *success*?' The householder bridled and ended the conversation. The Colonel was desolated. But very soon the painters were at work obliterating the hateful colours. 'Well, I liked it all right,' the householder explained, 'but I could see that the Colonel didn't, and he's such a nice old boy, I didn't want to upset him.'

Now I come to think of it, it is remarkable how many matters of high village policy are settled on those agreeable lines. Not all of them, of course. One day I may bring myself to record the great battle over the lopping of the churchyard lime-trees, in all its dark and litigious drama; but that may well be, as Sherlock Holmes said of the case of the Giant Rat of Sumatra, a story for which the world is not yet prepared.

FIVE

March is a rough old month, as my old neighbour habitually observes, but it has its good points. Every time the calendar's wheel revolves this far I think our forefathers were wise in holding it to be the true beginning of the new year, rather than some static, lifeless moment in January. However rough March may be, there comes a day when winter is at last seen to be in full retreat.

'Without Contraries,' as William Blake perceived, 'is no progression.' It is this deep law, no doubt, which accounts for the sense that something is amiss in those freakish years when a bland winter fades gently into a bland spring. We need to think of winter coming upon the scene with the panache of a rescuing cavalry charge; it is disappointing when there has been neither snow nor ice nor flood, and the winter slips away without any show of strength, and the forces of the spring gallop on to a field where the ancient enemy showed no disposition to make a stand. The times are out of joint if the soft airs of the Lenten days are only the merest advance upon the soft airs of winter.

To the old English who first colonised this valley March was the 'rough month', just as it is to my old friend; they called it *Hrethmonath*, the roughness thus denoted belonging to the sharp winds we can expect. Later they changed it, with burgeoning optimism perhaps, to *Length-monath*, the 'lengthening month', because in March the days perceptibly grow longer and the hours of darkness shrink; and if that is undoubtedly the more cheerful view to take, it is as well to remember the roughness as well.

On this Lady Day, March the twenty-fifth, which used to be the legal beginning of the year under the old dispensation, the sky was a flat and chilly grey which might have been left over from December. The birds, too, kept a wintry silence, responsive as usual at this season to the weather of the hour. A month ago, when the sun shone brightly for a few days, they sang in full voice, but today's relapse into winter had struck them dumb again. Even the rooks seemed to be at a loose end, hopping desultorily about the treetops with scarcely a croak between them.

As I squelched along the muddy path through the wood there was a mist in the air between the trees, and the sun was no more than a patch of pale yellow seen through the leafless branches. The right course on such a day is to turn the eye upon details. There is a greater variety of colours among the trees at this moment than there will be later when all is green, although the colours are present in innumerable minute particles instead of in dense masses. It is the time to look closely—at the silky, upward-pointing buds of the beech, the nutbrown blobs on the twigs of the oak, the tiny, bright red flowers protruding from green buds on the hazel, the red and yellow spots of growth upon the thorn. There are pleasures to be had best by those who have learned to look at small things as well as large. It is not necessarily those with the keenest eyes who master this lesson. Tennyson, who knew these particular pleasures (hence his many observant lines, such as 'More black than ashbuds at the front of

March'), learned it because his eyesight was poor; he was compelled to peer closely at objects and so saw them more clearly than others with sharper eyes.

There were indeed black ashbuds to be seen, fat and prosperous and sooty; but it was on the ground, under the trees and on the banks, that I found the chief signs of progress. Where, only the other day, had been a dun floor of fallen leaves, was now an expanse of fresh green growth. There were miniature nettles pushing up aggressive little scowling leaves; there were elegant outcrops of lords-and-ladies, not yet showing their insect-trapping heads, but in handsome leaf; there was ground ivy in abundance; and there were thick, soft drifts of dog's mercury, the ever-familiar plant of English woodland.

Why, I wonder, is this last plant so named? The answer would be found in that book which I have never yet discovered, because it would be impossible for anyone to write it—that book explaining the origins of all the remarkable names which have been acquired by wild flowers through the ages. Enchanter's Nightshade, Bugle, Yellow Archangel, Rocket, Baldmoney, Sweet Cicely, Don's Twitch . . . there would be no lack of subjects for its author. A lack of recorded knowledge from the days when the world was young, and plants were given their names, would be the difficulty. All I know of dog's mercury is that it is supposed to be poisonous to animals, and, offensive though this may be to a nation of dog-lovers, when 'dog' is attached to the name of a plant it is usually an indication that for some such reason it is held in disfavour.

I saw a pair of March hares loping and circling strangely on a ploughed hillside, endlessly turning and zig-zagging across the ground, driven on for who knows how many miles by the impulse of spring. Then I saw two kestrels who might almost have been mimicking the hares, high in the sky; it was like a curious aerial reflection of their restless pursuit, the hawks plunging and soaring around each other with that terrible mastery of the air which they command. Now and then the kestrels would separate to hover hungrily over the edge of the wood: play, and love-making, and then the merciless hunt, by turns: a reminder of Blake's 'Contraries' even when the weather seemed sunk in a flat monotony.

In the night we heard the stirrings of a wind, which grew into a gale, driving through the tall elms and chestnuts down the lane with a sound like a sea crashing against a shore. Next morning everything was different. The wind sang and roared through the branches, clouds went tumbling across a blue sky, and every living thing seemed to have been shaken into action. The rookery was in a state of turmoil, with black wings flapping wildly in the turbulent air, and everywhere birds were singing for dear life as if determined to make themselves heard above the racket. The hazel catkins no longer hung over the river with the stillness of an oriental painting; they gyrated madly above water rippling brilliantly before the wind. It was a day when the spring came upon us, not with gentle stirrings of the sap or visitations of soft airs, but with a fine, boisterous, reckless release of energy, taking the motionless winter world by storm, setting the skylarks singing and the dead leaves dancing and shaking out the dust and cobwebs of a season near its end.

Such a day in March can be the best of all days in the best of all months. For a time, that is. This is not, however, the season for moderation but for extremes. Instead of blowing itself out cheerfully and allowing us to relax after a bracing interlude, the gale grew stronger. It blew all day and into the night. I was awakened in the darkness by sounds of storm and fury, not a comfortable experience when the roof overhead has already endured the winds of several centuries. Occasionally a crash and a thud sounded in the din. I thought of the nearby trees and hoped for the best.

Next morning there were twigs and branches scattered across the ground in profusion and the drama was still in progress. The gale blew as hard as ever and bits were snapping off trees and shooting away in the wild air like misshapen arrows. Although walking was not comfortable, I made my way up the hill where the wind snarled in the treetops, in a sustained outpouring of noise which numbed the mind. I have heard that in parts of the world where strong winds blow uninterruptedly, the effect upon human beings is profound, and I can well believe it. So much strident power on the rampage could blow away a man's reason in time.

The rooks, on the other hand, appeared to be enjoying

themselves hugely, tumbling about in the gusts with abandon. Conditions looked far from easy in their nests, which were being heaved to and fro with a dizzy violence up aloft, swaying a dozen feet in each direction as the branches bent before the gale. Yet I suppose the birds were sitting snug upon their eggs, watching the world rock deliriously about them, for although their nests appear ramshackle and untidy from below, they always seem to hold firm in such a test. It was more than could be said for all the trees. Our lane was blocked to anything on wheels by the litter of torn branches scattered by the storm, and there was a bigger obstacle, too, the result of one of the heavier crashes which had sounded in the night. An elm, doomed perhaps in any case like so many of its kind, had toppled across the lane, smashing through a fence as it fell. Men from the council arrived with saws to clear it away, and people tottered through the mad air to shout their tales of other destructions at one another. Half a roof off, a favourite apple-tree ravaged, a henhouse blown to pieces; there was a story of a pony, terrified by the commotion, which had galloped blindly into the river and spent hours half-submerged.

The 'rough month' had shown its other face. After such a frenzy it would have been fitting if the storm had departed with a last and greatest burst of fury; but it just died away, leaving a sense of void. The lull before the storm is proverbial. I find the calm after a storm more impressive. We went out to collect armfuls of sticks for kindling. So much dead wood had come down that the pickings were as easy as manna to the children of Israel. The fallen tree lay beside the road in a solemn stillness: there was no hint of movement in the air, and a wren was flitting softly about the crushed branches. In the cathedral calm that prevailed, slanting columns of sunlight reached down from the treetops, and swarms of midges hovered in their warmth.

SIX

I almost trod upon a large brown hare today: a curious encounter with the shyest and fleetest of animals. A powerful-looking bundle of fur suddenly exploded under my feet and propelled itself through the air with a mighty leap. When it touched down again it fled across the field in a burst of panic speed.

If one is ever to take a hare by surprise it is sure to be in this season, when the spring fever, as has long been deduced from their erratic behaviour, makes them all mad. Nevertheless I wish I could keep a pet hare or two, as poor William Cowper did. The ways of hares are still mysterious in spite of the niggling thoroughness of modern naturalists, and part of their mystery is that creatures so wild and so timid should prove, when domesticated, to be so friendly to man. As Cowper wrote,

'It is no wonder that my intimate acquaintance with these specimens of the kind has taught me to hold the sportsman's amusement in abhorrence; he little knows what amiable creatures he persecutes, of what gratitude they are capable, how cheerful they are in their spirits, what enjoyment they have of life, and that, impressed as they seem with a peculiar dread of man, it is only because man gives them peculiar cause for it.'

It would be pleasant to convert the lonely fugitive of the fields into an 'amiable' and 'cheerful' member of the household, though I fear my spaniel would decline to co-operate.

At least there are plenty of hares to be seen in the open country, if not always at such close quarters as today. They were once even more numerous, but the odds nowadays are against the survival, in great numbers, of any animal so large and so noticeable. In Yorkshire I once came across at least fifty of them assembled in a moonlit field. My first thought was that they were the small north country sheep, an impression they dispelled by bounding off into the distance with most un-sheeplike speed. Today I seldom see more than a few at a time.

I saw other hares today, though, larking about in their crazy spring fashion. The hare's madness is, no doubt, only its own expression of the ancient folly which all the animal kingdom succumbs to when the sap is rising; nevertheless the males do go in for the most insane-seeming antics. They buck about like the wildest of kicking broncos, they bound over each other and try to inflict blows from midair with their powerful hind legs, they stage extraordinary boxing matches in which each participant sits up like a fighting kangaroo in a circus. At times they look ferocious. It is a strange show of ardour in a beast which in other respects is a by-word for a fearful melancholy, for although the hare is powerfully built, without its quivering watchfulness and its desperate speed it would be helpless before its enemies; yet it seems able to turn great reserves of pugnacity against its own kind in the stresses of the mating season.

I am not surprised that man's dealings with the hare, although generally of the harshest, should also have been accompanied throughout history by a touch of compassion. There is enough about the hare's place in the scheme of things to account for the idea of sadness which has always clung to it—its defencelessness, its attractions as meat for fiercer creatures, the loneliness of its life through most of the year. It was anciently thought, indeed, to be cursed with a peculiar sense of grief (which it was supposed to try to overcome by eating wild chicory, surely as lunatic a

34

notion as any the imagined madness of the hare has ever inspired).

Even its defensive gift of speed has been turned to its disadvantage through the ages, making it the favoured quarry of the hunt long before fox-hunting was thought of. In the days when the English forest was still unfelled, open country was largely a matter of the fields surrounding a village; beyond that stretched the greenwood, and anyone who tried to hunt a fox soon found that the chase petered out when the fox took refuge in the forest. The hare, however, knows no safety save in his own speed. When pursued he stays in the open. I could easily imagine the hare-hunting which took place on the slopes of this valley where today I found them disporting themselves, before the surrounding forest disappeared: a wide, circular gallop of hounds and quarry (for the hare often flees in circles when chased), with the tall trees ringing the scene to make a broad arena; and then the closing of the gap, and the kill, and the villagers' cheers. Hare coursing retained its high place among eighteenth-century country pursuits, as Parson Woodforde's journals make plain, and less than a century ago Wilfrid Scawen Blunt's Old Squire declared:

'I love the hunting of the hare
Better than that of the fox
I like to be as my fathers were
In the days ere I was born.'

Fox-hunting was a lowly business, a matter of keeping down vermin, when hunting the hare was accorded all the honours of the chase.

There is almost no end to the superstitions and odd beliefs about the hare. I still know people who think a hare's foot will bring them good luck or good health, just as Samuel Pepys used to believe. It was unlucky for a hare to cross your path, because witches changed themselves into hares when it suited them. People even had the strange idea that hares were sexless animals, or else that they changed their sex every year; a notion related to that characteristic which Sir Thomas Browne noted in his scholarly way and which he called '*Retromingency*, or pissing backward', a characteristic which might mislead observers, he explained; having seen both sexes 'to urine backward, or aversely between their legs, they might conceive there was a foeminine part in both'—wherein, he added, 'they are deceived'. I have no fresh light to throw either way upon that matter. Nevertheless it is strange to me that any countryman could have supposed hares to be sexless, and especially at this time of year, when they are battling with each other in continuous amorous frenzy.

It is always said that hares and rabbits will not share the same ground, even though they share much the same tastes in vegetarian diet. Doubtless this is true, although I fancy that the two species must be very nice in their drawing-up of demarcation lines. I have seen hares feeding surprisingly close to rabbits; they do not seem to need much distance between them to keep the peace. When the peace is broken, it is a violent matter. Rabbits are said to kill the young of intruding hares by biting their heads as they lie in the form. This intermittent warfare evidently explains the increase in the hare population after myxomatosis had begun to kill off the rabbits.

I saw more rabbits than hares today, however. For some years there has been talk in the village about the extent of the rabbits' revival, after they had been all but driven from the landscape by the plague. Country people have always found rabbits a great nuisance, and our forebears went to much trouble with traps and ferrets to keep them out of gardens and away from crops; but they at least found in the rabbits a compensating value to man to balance their hungry demands. Nowadays they are not even acceptable as meat, poor beasts. I can remember when most villages possessed some equivocal person who made a sort of living by trapping rabbits to sell for food (with a little extra to be had for the skins). Rabbit pie was a popular dish in countless households. That has pretty well gone now, as a result of myxomatosis and its horrors, and I know that I could not bring myself to eat rabbit again, not even the meat carefully labelled 'tame rabbit' which I sometimes see on sale in the market town.

It is unlucky for us that this general revulsion should have occurred when meat is getting scarcer in the world, and more expensive, because for a great many generations of country people the huge warrens which used to exist outside villages were important sources of meat. My wife has a copy of Mrs

Beeton's original cookery book, published in 1861, and in it I find many pages of rabbit recipes. They make me rather queasy, the least appetising of all being the starkly named 'Boiled Rabbit'; its ingredients are listed, with horrid simplicity, as 'Rabbit, water'.

A rabbit warren today is usually on a fairly small scale, but warrens used to cover large acreages. The output of rabbit-meat from such breeding-grounds must have been vast, certainly enough to make it a significant part of the diet of the rural poor, especially as it could be got for nothing by any skilful man, whether the landowner approved or not. Quite often the land-owner did not approve. There is a strain of meanness running through the modern history of the relations between land-owners and the people, a strain which reached its ugliest at the time of the Enclosures and thereafter, and local tyrants' edicts banning the catching of rabbits were in this tradition. But of course these edicts were, sensibly, disregarded.

Of the numerous ways of catching rabbits which I have heard of, the most remarkable was with the aid of a toad and a stub of candle. The candle was fixed to the back of the toad and lit; then the toad was sent crawling down a rabbit hole, and the shock of seeing a light advancing into their stronghold was enough to send rabbits flying out into the open to be captured. I think if our present-day rabbits multiply as it seems they might, they will be dealt with in less imaginative, but more thorough, ways; although I think enough will always survive to preserve the species.

Although I admire the rabbit's tenacious grip upon life, the hare is to my mind the more engaging creature. It is with him that my sympathies lie in the war between the species. Hares range around the land, rabbits move in regiments and dig them-selves in like infantry; they are the Roundheads to the hares' Cavaliers.

And then, the hare is almost the only wild animal in these islands which shows a willingness to challenge man, a para-doxical but appealing characteristic in a creature which is proverbially frightened and elusive. It does so on its own terms, it is true; the fact remains that, depending as it does for its very life upon its wonderful speed, it sometimes seems to take such

37

pride in its prowess that it will throw down a daring challenge to man. I have often come across a hare when I am driving and have seen him delay in the road until the car was close enough for me to see him in full detail—whiskers, black eartips and all—before taking off with a surge of acceleration. He could easily dart to one side or the other but he propels himself straight down the middle of the road: a challenge! It seems to be the same spirit which causes large numbers of hares to congregate at airports in various parts of the world and set themselves to run wild races with the aircraft moving over the ground. Speed is life to the hare. I am pleased to think that, surrounded as he is by unceasing hostility, he sometimes glories in his own unique powers, in the thrill of a challenge and a race.

SEVEN

The cowslips were standing up in the soft, wet grass in the fields this morning, sparkling with dew. One meadow is dotted with the pale lilac heads of the cuckoo-flowers, which with faultless punctuality have shown themselves just as the cuckoo itself has announced its return. There used to be a patch of these delicate beauties in the churchyard, but they have been extinguished by excess of gardening zeal, a sad case of extermination by motor-mower. In the same way the grassy banks beside the lanes have in many places lost their power to stage a blissful flower show for us each spring. The council sends a man with a clanking machine to gobble up the lot and spew it out again as a soft green mush. It might be worse. Many councils show their local pride by spraying poisons wholesale beside their roads.

The fields, though, are full of life, with skylarks sounding incessantly in a sky of pale blue and shimmering white. The morning had a hint of zestful coolness in the air in spite of the sun. I set myself the task of trying to catch sight of the cuckoo, never an easy thing to do at will. The voice is inescapable, the bird itself likes to lurk out of view. 'Still longed for, never seen'—Wordsworth knew the difficulty, and he had a fondness for cuckoos some might think rather at variance with the strict morality of his later years.

I heard the Wandering Voice sound clearly and crisply from the edge of a wood as I approached; which is to say, I thought it came from there, but soon, and not for the first time, I began to suspect the cuckoo of playing ventriloquial tricks. He was not to be seen when I reached the spot and there was no glimpse of him darting away to avoid me. A few minutes later he began to call again from the other side of the wood. I changed direction, to the irritation of a party of wood-pigeons who had to rise noisily through the branches at my approach. There was not another human being in sight, nor any human habitation, but the country was full of movement and sound. The hedges were busy with bees and guarded at every few yards by singing birds. One had a sense of a great stirring of life, only a fraction of the process being visible or audible, the rest of it happening with irresistible force unseen: unmistakably there, like the cuckoo, but more a presence in the air than a solid, identifiable fact.

Perhaps the sensible thing to do was to rest for a little, to see if the cuckoo passed in view, instead of pursuing him like a fool in a travesty of a hunt which gave the quarry all the advantages. I went ahead to a gate where last year, as I suddenly remembered, I had seen not one but two cuckoos. They had sped past at their usual express rate and the female had sounded her extraordinary call, a bubbling, chuckling, skittish effusion quite unlike the cuckoo-clock mockery of the male. I leaned against the gate, watched a couple of rabbits hopping about in the grass and followed the lordly passage of a kestrel across the sky. But no cuckoo came. His voice, even, dropped out of the chorus.

No matter. I had come to the parish 'springs', the scattered line of woods which extend along the western boundary like leafy frontier posts. The trees spread a soft green haze overhead, with pools of primroses underneath. The crowing of a pheasant, a little way off, echoed among the trees and a sweet April calm reigned. 'Spring' is the old word for a coppice. Each of these has its own name as well: Rectory Spring, Piddock's Spring, Bunter's Spring, linking each patch of coppiced timber with a house down in the village. The names are reminders of the importance which coppicing once possessed in the self-contained economy of the parish, 'spring' being a plain enough label for the endless process of cutting-down and springing-up which coppicing involves.

Someone had been harvesting the timber crop. There was a tidy pile of trimmed poles in a cleared space within the coppice. The work had evidently been done in the old way, except no doubt for the labour-saving power-saw. The gnarled hazel stumps, the 'stools' as they are called, had sent up a group of strong young shoots since the last felling, and these had now been removed; after another decade or so has passed, there will be another cluster of growth to gather from them. That was the ancient pattern. By cutting a tenth of the coppice each year, the owner obtained a steady supply of wood for poles, fencing, stakes, fuel and all the other uses for which it was indispensable.

These springs are themselves fairly ancient, as one can tell not only by the aged aspect of the stools, but because they appear on the oldest maps of the district. They have stood here through many a ten-year cycle of growth and harvest. Today, when everything favours intensive cultivation and quick returns, there are not many cases of cropping being organised on a time-scale as long as a decade. Earlier generations lived within a different system of continuities. Some coppices were interspersed with successive plantings of oaks, to ensure a continuous supply of mature oak timber; and as oaks flourish for centuries, that was indeed an interdependence between past, present and future.

The springs are a couple of miles outside the village. There must have been heavy work for horses dragging the wood down the rough track which I had followed, delectable path though it was for me on this cuckoo morning. But how important it was, when fuel was precious and timber an all-important material for work! We tend, in our parochial way, to think present-day anxieties over fuel and its price represent a unique misfortune, but when fuel had to be found on the local patch of earth there was plenty to worry about. The well-off, with their own coppices and ample cheap labour available, managed comfortably enough, but the poor often went cold, sitting around their 'shivering hearth' as Disraeli depicted them in *Sybil*. William Cobbett writes of one place where 'the poor take by turns the making of fires at their houses to boil four or five tea-kettles. What a winter-life must these lead, whose turn it is not to make the fire!' Elsewhere he saw villagers carrying home bean and wheat stubble to use for fuel; any dried vegetation that would give out a little heat was of value. The enclosures made the shortages acute, by cutting off the people's rights to gather fuel on lands that had once been common; so did the advance of agricultural knowledge, in many places, for a common English household fuel had been 'bricks' made from cow-dung mixed with straw, and these came to be seen as robbing the land of good manure. Only the arrival of the railways, which carried coal, ended the fuel scarcity in the countryside.

A single-track railway line came down this valley in Queen Victoria's later years and the coppices at once began to lose their importance. The line passed only a few hundred yards away from them. I could see its course, bending away to the north to connect three other villages higher up the valley before coming to a stop. Until a few years ago a train trundled up and down several times a day; the locomotive was permanently attached to the southern end of the set of carriages, and when it travelled north it pushed them from behind. Then the entire branch was lopped off by the Beeching axe. It had outlived its usefulness, we were told. The rails were torn up and the cuttings and embankments abandoned to the rabbits and the foxes.

I moved on to another old coppice, one which has been neglected for years. This was once planted with hornbeams by some now-forgotten village worthy, and these, instead of being cut down regularly to ground level, have long been left to do as they pleased. As a result the place has a faintly fantastic air; most of the trees have grown tall, but they have assumed unnatural, convoluted shapes on the way. They look as if they had not known quite how to proceed when, after having been denied their normal upright growth for so long, they were at last left to themselves. Last month's great gale had brought down a heavy fall of broken branches and even a couple of trees had collapsed, leaning stricken against their neighbours. The little wood, with its tree-trunks writhing strangely upwards and with a litter of destruction around their roots, looked haunted and forlorn.

But out in the sunshine the cuckoo was calling again. I thought I saw him up in the branches of an ash-tree, still bare amid the surrounding new-green foliage, but it proved to be only a pigeon giving himself airs.

All was warm and summerlike as I came back to the village. The gardens looked as if they had been brushed and combed and told to sit up straight. I went past the cottage of my old neighbour and he, of course, was standing by his gate, where he is to be found during most of the hours of daylight. It serves him as a lookout post and as a convenient point for social intercourse. We exchanged observations upon the excellent weather, and he politely accepted the customary compliments upon the robust health of everything growing in his garden. The cuckoo was still calling somewhere not far off. 'That old cuckoo bird just flew down here,' said the old man. 'Went down the lane past your house.' Maddening bird: or rather (Wordsworth was right again) 'No bird, but an invisible thing, A voice, a mystery'.

EIGHT

Bird's-nesting is not as popular with country boys as it used to be, which we should doubtless be glad about, for there are more than enough threats to the common and the uncommon birds alike without young ruffians grabbing their eggs. I remember the patiently acquired collections which were objects of pride in my schooldays, containing eggs of dozens of species, all carefully 'blown' and laid out in cases lined with cotton wool. It was a deplorable hobby; but it did depend upon a kind of easy familiarity with wild life which is unusual nowadays, when either the young are earnest ornithologists in the making or else never give the subject a thought.

I never went in for egg-collecting but I loved finding nests. I still do. It would be a reproach to a misspent life, I dare say, to compute how many hours I have spent prowling along hedges or meandering over open ground, eyes down, in the search. The first nest of the year is still a point of some moment in the calendar; this year it was that of a robin, a finely woven little lair insinuated into a crevice in an elm-tree bole, and from a cautious distance I have watched the reddish-brown eggs hatch into a brood of fledglings.

Even without birds' nests to look for, the hedges would be a joy at this season, fresh and brilliant in their new foliage and shining in the sun. I try not to think of the desolation that will be bequeathed to posterity if the modern farmer's hatred of hedges is allowed to express itself to the bitter end, with the land scraped bare like the surface of the moon; neither do I believe that this will really happen; I keep an irrational belief that as long as there is an English countryside, there will be hedges. And for us in this parish, hedges mean hawthorns; the hedgerows contain other species in abundance, from the blackthorn which supplies us with sharp little fruits to the holly we collect at Christmas, but it is the thorn which rules.

The first hawthorn flowers appeared one showery morning, a mere handful of white pellets hanging from a sunny hedge-corner on the hillside. Next day the multitudinous buds had opened everywhere into full may blossom, and the hedges were half-hidden by great, billowing drifts of flower. The transformation was sudden and splendid. No wonder the tree was regarded as the emblem of hope, and its branches carried in wedding processions long ago, since it makes so dazzling a show of the vigour of the life force. And we know, of course, that may blossom has always been linked with the celebrations of spring, in pagan and Christian times alike.

There is, nevertheless, a certain puzzle about this ritual use, especially the tradition that hawthorn garlands were the essential decoration of the maypole during the free-and-easy festivities of May Day. It is a question of timing. The spring weather this year has been no more severe than average, yet the month of

May was well advanced before the hawthorns burst into their prodigal blossoming; and I have often noticed that May Day has come and gone long before the may blossom is out. This makes little difference to me; it never seems to matter much whether these seasonal landmarks come over the horizon early or late, provided they do not fail; but for the master of ceremonies in a May Day carnival it must have been awkward, or worse, if the principal ritual object habitually failed to supply itself on time. One might conclude that the climate has deteriorated since the days of Merry England. I suppose this is possible, although the old men grumble that in this topsy-turvy modern world, winters are nothing like so hard as they used to be. I prefer to find an explanation in the fact that May Day was dislocated by the calendar reform of 1752. Perhaps that disturbance in the familiar order of things, when mobs ran through the streets shouting, 'Give us back our eleven days!', was rather like our present-day fads of metrication and decimalisation, stirring up similar public feelings of irritation and then acquiescence, and like them leaving behind small scars upon ordinary life. One of these scars was that May Day happened eleven days earlier, so that thereafter hawthorns were hardly ever in blossom on their appointed day.

The hawthorn makes a good-sized tree if given the chance. Usually it is kept down to hedge size, a reduced rôle to which it adapts itself readily; it was the rare adaptability of the thorn which caused it to be used as the almost invariable hedging-plant at the time of the Enclosures, when landowners found themselves under legal obligation to put in thousands of miles (that is no exaggeration) of fencing or hedging. But when it is allowed space and time it grows to handsome stature. A favourite path of mine at this time of year leads across a series of meadows deep in buttercups and clover, and with a scatter of fully-grown hawthorn trees standing to the right and to the left. Sometimes, particularly when the sun is shining after a shower, the fragrance is almost unbelievable. The famous scents of the Corsican *maquis* are not a scrap more delightful or more pervasive. These seductive odours have a powerful attraction for the honey-bees, good judges in these matters. 'To scent the skies, and purge th'unwholesome air'—that was how Dryden saw the

46

task of the hawthorn. Who cares whether it comes early or late, so long as it comes?

There is no disguising the fact that a great many hedges have been grubbed up in the past decade or so, however, making the average field a good deal bigger than it used to be. I have the impression that the surviving hedges are more populous as a result. A hedge of the old style, dense and impenetrable and with a variety of different trees and shrubs interspersed among the thorn, fairly pulsates with bird life nowadays. Bird populations fluctuate according to the availability of food and shelter, I know, but they will not contract without some effort at resistance. When a favoured hedgerow or thicket disappears, I guess there must be much jostling and rivalry for space in all other suitable places nearby. The territorial birds can afford a certain amount of flexibility in the size of their private patches. I know a few ancient and unkempt hedges in this parish which seem to be teeming with small birds just now, with a non-stop scurrying and fluttering in the branches.

Many birds do live at closer quarters than we are tempted to suppose. The fact conflicts with sentimental ideas about the freedom of the birds, but there it is. Take the skylark, that 'bird of the wilderness, Blithesome and cumberless', as a memorably bad poem has it, which, with or without the aid of tongue-twisting couplets, is often seen as a symbol of happy liberty. The more one considers its life, the more one realises that the truth is by no means as simple as that.

The whole countryside is loud with skylarks at the moment. I could walk for mile upon mile, hour after hour, without ever leaving the sound of the singing larks in the sky. No other birds sing with such profusion and extravagance, not even in this island which is so full of pleasing noises. Even the cuckoo, after haunting and mocking the traveller for a time, falls dumb or moves out of earshot, whereas the lark is seldom silent during the hours of daylight, and long before you have walked out of the range of one of them you have entered the territories of others. Going across skylark country is like moving beneath a series of overlapping cones of song, each cone having at its apex a fluttering speck which continues to rise vertically in the air long after it has ceased to be visible.

47

On a fine fresh morning it would be the easiest thing in the world to persuade oneself that the reason for all this was the sheer pleasure of life and the joy of singing in a blue sky. To human ears there is a singularly jubilant or exultant quality in the lark's song. It is made up of a great variety of calls and notes poured out at torrential speed; none of these sounds would attract much attention if uttered in isolation, but when sent down to earth in a brilliant cascade their effect is electrifying. He would be an odd person whose spirits did not lift at the sound. From that it is a short step to fancying that the sense of elation is shared with its originator up in the sky.

It will not do, though. What the skylark is really about, as he carols his way into the blue, is demarcating his territory and warning off intruders of his own kind; just like any other song-birds, except that they perch on branches to sing, whereas there are no branches in the open spaces which the lark frequents. With neither lookout posts nor singing-stands available, he has to make them himself out of the air with those powerful, pointed wings.

If you watch him for a time you see that he is not, in fact, singing incessantly, 'blithesome and cumberless', but is making fairly frequent swoops to drive off intruders. And if you listen to the song at close quarters (which can be done, although it is not exactly easy) much of that familiar element of carefree pleasure seems to be missing; it sounds harsher and more strident. Perhaps this is closer to what it sounds like to another skylark. When wandering over a countryside where no other human figure is in view it is easy to forget that for many creatures, notably skylarks, this is not a place of wide and empty spaces but a congested area, where the competition for breeding space is intense, and where a tract of territory once held has to be defended with incessant effort.

I suppose there are some for whom this sort of knowledge dims their pleasure in the lark's song or their admiration at its tireless ascent towards the sun. It does not do so for me. The truth is at least as remarkable as the sentimental idea, indeed more so than the notion of songbirds as mere makers of sets of agreeable noises, like amateur pianists too limited in technique to master new works. Besides, whatever intensity of purpose and life-or-death determination prompt the lark's song, it still sounds matchless and thrilling to the human ear.

NINE

There are daisies in the lawn as thick as leaves in autumn. If I were a different kind of gardener I should be ashamed of them. I am conscious of two principal schools of thought among gardeners. Adherents of one school are content to restrict their efforts to the general encouragement of nature along the lines she is inclined in the ordinary course of things to follow; the others work in a more masterful way, as if the true art of the gardener lay in the creation of a miniature alternative to the natural order, in which nothing grows quite as it would if left to its own resources. There is much to be said for both schools. One produces idealised versions of the English landscape, the other achieves triumphs of formal discipline and horticultural expertise.

My own place, without a doubt, is in some lowly corner of the first category. The matter was crystallised for me today during a visit from a gardening friend of the more austere sort. We sat on the garden seat in the sunshine and looked at the patch of lawn,

'trim with daisies pied' as Milton had it, and while I was thinking how pleasant it was to enjoy such a profusion of flowers with
so little effort, he was taking a different view. 'You really will
have to clear those daisies out of the lawn,' he said after a time.
I saw his point, of course, and I share the general admiration
for a smooth greensward; but since the handsome carpet of
daisies is there, I think I shall leave them in peace. I could spray
poison on them, and spread fertiliser, and re-seed the grass, and
so on, but I do not feel any desire to do so. Mine is not that sort
of garden: and laziness reinforces the inclination to leave well
alone. In such a case it is a convenience to have a sketchy theory
about the duality of gardening to buttress one's position.

This is the high season for visiting other people's gardens. It
is a variable experience, I have found, especially when one is the
host rather than the visitor. It is one thing to have summer
guests from the city looking round, without too much expert
knowledge to blunt their admiration, but callers such as my
expert friend of today have a way of turning a visit into a more
testing, and humbling, encounter. His gardening is on that high
level which enables him, from time to time, to charge members
of the public for the privilege of inspecting his achievements;
ostensibly this is to raise funds for district nurses, or the repair of
the church roof, or some other unexceptionable purpose, but I
suspect the cause most generously served by his 'open days' is
his own innocent pride. As he went the rounds today it was not
long before gently wounding remarks began to mingle with the
polite approval. 'Well, the black spot isn't quite so bad this
year,' he would say encouragingly as we looked at the roses; or,
'Those ericas are pretty good, considering the soil conditions.'
It is hard to convince these perfectionists that one positively
likes having daisies in the lawn.

On the whole I prefer looking at other people's gardens to
showing off my own. Often they yield ideas which can be
appropriated; but, more than that, I like to see the differing
ways in which people interpret the potentialities of their own
pieces of ground. What a man makes of his garden says much
about his nature and his aspirations. It reveals him as a classicist
or a romantic, as slapdash or meticulous, as ambitious or diffi-
dent; it discloses to one glance more about himself than he would

51

readily supply in much conversation. A garden is an auto-biography, for those who can read the language.

There are also gardens which are autobiographical records in another sense, those gardens whose owners have the amiable habit of collecting plants and cuttings from friends; over the years these garnerings acquire something of the character of a photograph album, the charm of which is its power to summon up forgotten or half-forgotten people and places. Our village doctor has his own private variation upon this theme. 'My garden is full of patients,' he sometimes says, whereupon guests have been known to peer about them curiously, wondering whether some epidemic has caused the waiting-room to overflow down the paths and lawns and among the flower-beds. Not so: the doctor, in the quarter of a century during which he has trans-formed a bare field into a mellow and delightful garden, has received small gifts of plants and shrubs from many friends to whom he has been of professional service. Thus, he looks at his flourishing willow-tree and thinks of Mrs X's first baby; his beech hedge puts him in mind of a local farmer's slipped disc; quite a few items, being tokens of gratitude from bereaved families, recall neighbours and patients who are now beyond need of his medical endeavours. I wonder if any other country doctor possesses this sort of casebook within his garden. It is hardly an example the rest of us could copy, of course. If I heard my overwhelmingly expert friend say that my garden was full of patients, I should know at once that he was alluding not to the grateful providers but to the state of health of what was growing there.

Yet sometimes I yearn for grandeur in a garden. The thought came to me the other day, during a visit to the property of one of our most affluent inhabitants, that of all garden luxuries the one I would most like to possess is a walk of pleached limes. It belongs with such spaciously elegant pleasures as ancient cedars set in spreading lawns, or a sweep of meadow and woodland viewed from one's terrace across a ha-ha. The very words 'pleached limes' have a silken, musical sound: how delicious to stroll or to sit, on a hot summer's day, in such a cool green shade.

And how strange that no one nowadays seems to take the trouble to create such a place. Rich men spend lavishly upon their country houses and their gardens, but usually with an eye to quick returns. Patience, and a generous impulse towards posterity, are out of fashion; the long view of a garden-artist like Capability Brown or any of his lesser followers, none of whom can have seen their works of landscape gardening attain their best, is seldom evident. Yet I would expect anyone who takes pleasure in growing things to derive as much satisfaction from watching something grand and durable coming into being as from the customary concentration upon short-term ventures. My friend's pleached limes were planted by his grandfather, and his memory is often honoured as a consequence.

This word 'pleach' seems to be related to 'plait', which fairly accurately explains its meaning, and also to 'plash'; since the Middle Ages, at least, it has described the process of training and bending the branches of a tree or hedge so that it grows into a living screen of whatever size and shape is required. To plash a hedge is to 'lay' it, as we say now, cutting the stems half-through and intertwining them; and to pleach trees is to treat them in a rather similar way, pruning away unwanted branches and training the rest over a frame of poles and wire, with a result that exists happily half-way between architecture and gardening.

I do not suppose many trees would put up with this treatment. The lime, however, is the most obliging of trees, a quality which it shows in various ways. The French make a *tisane* or infusion of the flowers, which I have tasted in France and found pleasant enough; I remember there was an attempt during the last war to persuade people to try it to eke out the tea ration, but it made no headway against our insular habits. There used to be an industry of making mats from the inner bark of the lime, which was shredded and twisted to produce a material rather like rush. And then, its wood is perfect for the carver. Grinling Gibbons invariably employed it. It is even said to be resistant to woodworm. But the lime-tree's obligingness is most marked in its tolerance of this ancient process of pleaching, for it may be pruned and trimmed and shaped and trained almost without limit, and still it will flourish. Given its head, it makes a large and lofty tree, altogether unlike the lime-tree walk's closely-planted rows with their branches disciplined and interlaced to form a leafy tunnel. It seems to get on equally well in either situation.

53

The July sun has brought the lime-trees into flower. The bees fall upon the flowers in buzzing multitudes, and sometimes they gorge themselves so greedily that they fall stupefied to the ground. This may even be one of those years when, it is said, the lime's nectar is so potent that it has an unusually narcotic effect upon them; in such vintage years only the bees with strong heads, so to speak, can handle the stuff; but those are the years when the lime flower honey is superlative.

Coleridge wrote a poem called 'This Lime Tree Bower My Prison' on a day when, because 'dear Sara had upset a skillet of boiling milk' upon his foot, he had to sit in the garden bower instead of going off walking with the Wordsworths and Charles Lamb. He begins on a note of complaint, but he ends serenely. It would have been odd, in such happy conditions of confinement, if he had not.

When I have furnished my ideal, noble garden with its pleached limes, I move on in my mind through the adjacent pleasure-spaces, one opening from another like the great apartments at Versailles; and then I stroll across the spreading lawns to take in the view, between towering trees, of parkland and woods and distant hills, all seen uninterruptedly by the grace of that happy invention, the ha-ha.

There are few amenities more seductive in these cramped and congested times than the green spaciousness conjured up by the ha-ha, as it links large vistas of open countryside to the domesticated environs of a country house, without visible barrier. The idea of a sunken fence is, besides, pleasing in its nice blend of simplicity and ingenuity. Once someone had thought of it, others must have found it an obvious enough idea. I do not know, with any certainty, who had the first flash of inspiration, although the credit is often given to William Kent, that painter, architect and father of landscape gardening who did so much to change the look of England in the early years of the eighteenth century. He 'leapt the fence', in the words of Horace Walpole, 'and found all nature was a garden'. Nevertheless the ha-ha probably originated on the Continent and may well have been first suggested by the use of ditches and sunken obstacles in fortifications. Its name is also borrowed from the French, who had called it in this way because 'Ha!' was what people were supposed to exclaim in their surprise at coming across the oddity of a fence hidden in a ditch; which sounds a trifle implausible, but then etymology so often does.

The interesting historical fact is that the innovation of the ha-ha, which permitted the garden to be married to the surrounding landscape without impediment, came when new ideas were stirring, and the English were rebelling against excessive artificiality and contrivance in their gardens. This was Addison's complaint:

'Our British Gardeners . . . instead of humouring Nature, love to deviate from it as much as possible. Our trees rise in Cones, Globes and Pyramids. We see the Marks of the Scissars upon every Plant and Bush . . . I would rather look upon a Tree in all its Luxuriancy and Diffusion of Boughs and Branches, than when it is thus cut and trimmed into a Mathematical Figure.'

Behind that mild protest there lay a revolution in taste. From it sprang that ideal, which persists still in the English imagination, of a garden which is an Eden-like version of nature rather than a mere artefact.

That, I suppose, is why my perfect garden must have its ha-ha. But if I attach myself, in imagination, to that ideal, I favour a certain catholicity in practice. I do not, at the moment, wholeheartedly echo Addison's commination of the 'Marks of the Scissars' because, while sticking in general to the *laissez-faire* approach to gardening which I have described, I have also begun to experiment with its opposite, which is topiary, the clipping of bushes into shapes which cannot possibly exist within nature's scheme of things.

I have often taken pleasure in the sculptural effect of lovingly trimmed box or yew, provided that the topiarist's fancy has not led him into Disneyesque vulgarities. When I found that an old (and untrimmed) box-tree had presented me with several thriving seedlings in one flower-bed, I thought I would try my hand at a little closely-disciplined gardening for a change. Since the first requirement seemed to be advice on how to go about it, I consulted a man in the village who has the authority in the matter conferred by a hedge from which arise one clipped peacock and several geometrical forms. He told me that what was needed was patience, an answer which was illuminating in a way, but not directly helpful. However, I transplanted, and clipped hopefully with a pair of scissors, and the midget shrubs are now beginning to show some resemblance (given a little latitude of imagination) to the dense, green spheres which will one day, as I hope, stand at nicely-chosen points in the garden. I now understand the fascination of that Japanese craft of producing miniature versions of forest trees. There came a moment of discouragement when I found that a local nurseryman was offering well-grown, ready-made specimens of topiary at what seemed rather reasonable prices; but I persuaded myself that the satisfaction of doing the thing oneself was all-important, and that buying topiary off the peg would be little better than ordering books by the yard.

Now I look at the slowly forming green shapes of my bushes and feel, in the faintest way, the tug of temptation. From my playing about with these diminutive box seedlings, the wildest megalomaniac ideas might sprout. I remember how Alexander Pope, while creating his little walks and arbours at Twickenham, conceived a mad, grand project for remodelling an entire mountain, in emulation of a classical plan to refashion Mount Athos as a stupendous effigy of Alexander. 'If anybody would make me a present of a Welsh mountain,' he wrote, 'I would undertake to see it executed . . . The figure must be in a reclining posture, because of the hollowing that would otherwise be necessary . . . It should be a rude unequal hill, and might be helped with groves of trees for the eyebrows, and wood for the hair . . .' I fear that is the sort of afflatus we topiarists are prey to, as we fiddle with our twigs and scissors.

TEN

An unsettling report passed through the village and it seemed best to go straight down to the 'Fox and Hounds' to verify it. Yes, said the landlord, as he let my pint of beer flow gently into the mug from the barrel behind the bar, it was true. He had told the brewery that he did not intend to renew his tenancy when the present five-year term ran out, so in a matter of weeks he and his wife would pack up. We shall have to adjust to a newcomer and his ways—provided, that is, that someone is found to take on the old pub. If not, one more village inn will close its doors as so many others have done in recent years. The thought lingered sombrely in the quiet bar parlour.

It was one of those hot summer evenings when no one seems to stir in the village. The pub door stood open and the roses basked in the sun. There were swallows darting and swooping gracefully in the warm air and, further off, I could see a party of swifts wheeling like demons around the church tower. Otherwise the scene seemed given over to stillness, the stillness of a pleasant summer fatigue when a draught of cool beer in a shady pub adds a lustre to the hour.

The trouble was, said the landlord, that the brewery had told him they meant to put up the rent by an awkwardly large sum. We told him we would be sorry to see him go, but when he mentioned the figure, we said we could not blame him. Neither, for that matter, had the man from the brewery who had given him the bad news: in fact, he appeared to think it the only sensible decision. The impression he gave was that the day of the small country pub was coming to an end; his own company expected to close down scores of them in the next few years. It will pay them better to sell off the buildings for conversion into private houses.

The landlord, however, was reassuring about our own prospects. He thought somebody would come along convinced that he could pay the new rent for the 'Fox and Hounds' and still make a fair living out of it, and that would provide for a few more years at least. It turned out that he had already had a number of prospective tenants looking around, not all of them particularly promising in the rôle of village innkeeper, it was true, but he was sure something would turn up.

One military-looking person had walked round the place and after examining the minute dining-room and the little batch of bedrooms upstairs had begun to question the landlord. 'You have a good chef?' he inquired pleasantly. 'Well, a good cook, not a chef,' said mine host. 'And how many in the kitchen altogether?' 'Two,' he was told. 'And how many do you have looking after the bedrooms?' A pause: then, 'Two,' he was told again. 'And how many to run the bar?' A longer pause. 'Two,' came the reply eventually. 'Ah, excellent. Six altogether, then.' 'No,' said the landlord. 'Two altogether. Me and the wife.' It will be a surprise if any more is heard of him. He left saying that he had no wish to run such a place without an adequate staff; whereupon he was told that in that case he had better find some other outlet for his talents, since the 'Fox and Hounds' had been advertising for a bit of help on Saturday nights for some months, without response, and apart from that the takings could not conceivably be enlarged to support the sort of labour force he had in mind.

I suppose he was one of that familiar breed of amateurs in the trade—men who, forced to find some new occupation in middle life, think it would be fun to run a village pub. Doubtless he had a pleasant picture of himself pottering amiably into the bar, exchanging agreeable gossip with a few favoured customers, and pottering out again to improve his garden or to wander off in search of a trout or two for breakfast. The reality, alas, is not like that. The publican has to work long and hard, and our present man tells me that in five years he has had only one week's holiday, and that was not achieved without much trouble in finding somebody to run things while he was away. What is more, since there is little profit to be made out of a few village people dropping in for the odd pint of an evening, his wife has to work equally hard on the food and bedroom side of the business.

All the same, it seems damnable that so many village pubs, which serve their communities well, should be fading out of existence. People drink at least as much as ever they did, and spend far more money in the process—yet the ancient institution of the inn can do no more than struggle to survive, especially in those small and isolated villages where it is most needed. There never was a clearer case of economic forces combining to frustrate the general will. I dare say the dogmas of economics say this is impossible, but if we have learned anything at all in recent years, it is that economics, quite as much as the law was in Mr Bumble's eyes, is 'a ass—a idiot'.

In many cases the breweries, with their horrible background music and their depraved ideas of interior decoration, seem eager to efface the memory, even, of what a proper country pub should be like. This often extends to the stuff they sell as beer. The philistines have spared neither the places nor the beverage. I do not pretend to any great connoisseurship in the matter, but I happen to have the advantage that I have tasted beer, if not at its absolute best, at any rate of an excellence to shame the froth off the gaseous, mean-spirited stuff the beer-factories of today produce. It was as different from that as is home-baked bread

59

from the cardboard loaves of the modern baking industry.

When I think of it I return mentally to one scorching August day of my boyhood, in that distant England of the nineteen-thirties which I have already recalled. I was walking with my father along a lonely Pennine valley. We were being grilled by an unusual northern heatwave, there was dust hanging in the air over the scorched moorland road, and the flies were infuriating. Then a moment arrived when he suggested, in cheerful tones which broke most welcomely into the sweating silence, that we should abandon the direct route to turn down a steep by-road to a certain village. When we arrived there he headed for a small and, as I remember it, decrepit pub, and my mind filled with thoughts of lemonade or ginger beer. My father knew better. It turned out that this was one of the few surviving inns, even in that remote epoch, at which home-brewed beer was still made and sold. He asked for some of this and the inn-keeper, a taciturn old man who looked as if he spent more time on the moors than in the bar-parlour, banged down two empty mugs on the table and filled them from a tall enamel jug.

Although I was too young to care much for beer at the time I can recall with extreme clarity the experience of lifting that golden, fragrant drink to my parched lips. It was a magnificent tipple, cool and nutty and ripely flavoured; if the white-washed walls of the little inn did not quiver to the sound of celestial violins as it went down, they came as near to doing so as made no difference. I stared at the empty mug in my hands and felt a delicious glow of well-being. My father, thinking perhaps that the landlord might belatedly remember that there were such things as licensing laws, or else recalling that we still had some miles to walk, refrained from ordering a refill for me, although mere politeness demanded that he should himself consume another pint. Before we left we were permitted to inspect the brewhouse where the wonderful stuff was made. The landlord spoke hardly at all but accepted our grateful praise as his due.

That was a happy enough encounter. But for years thereafter, a barrel of home-brewed beer would from time to time appear at home, whenever, I imagine, the transport could conveniently be arranged. It varied slightly in quality, as do the productions of all great artists, but it never fell below the level of excellence.

60

Today, looking back over the years at this fountain of nectar, I can see that for me it was not a stroke of altogether unalloyed good fortune, because it set a standard for beer which hardly anything has subsequently been able to attain. That corner of life has been, so to speak, downhill all the way, as if one had imbibed freely of Château Latour in youth only to discover that the nearest available equivalent in later years was a rough red plonk.

Well, it has all gone now, vanished from the earth like the wine that Odysseus drank, or the sack which nourished the mighty laughter of Falstaff. However, the other day a hospitable neighbour took me into the kitchen of his farmhouse and poured me a glass of ale. To say that it matched that brew of years ago would be to go too far, but it, too, produced sensations of delight and surprise. It was, my friend explained, a home-brewed beer which his wife had long been producing, and which they modestly thought was now of a quality to merit its being offered to friends. We toasted her industry and good sense in several more glasses.

It is surely a reproach to the brewers that this business of making beer at home should have grown so fashionable in recent years, however praiseworthy the practice may be in itself. There is a shop in our local town which has many shelves stacked with ingredients and utensils for the purpose. Some people buy substances in cans and merely carry out the final processes, others begin with the barley and the hops and follow the happy sequence from start to finish. I imagine much of the beer produced is sad stuff but some of it, as I have found out for myself, is marvellous. Presumably this fashion, like the parallel one for home-made wine, is a sign of the prevalent hankering, in the Plastic Age, for the real or imagined pleasures of our rural past, when wine-making and brewing were as everyday a part of the domestic round as cooking or baking. Expense is also an important consideration and this must be particularly so in the case of wine; for the truth is that most of the home-made wines I have tasted, whether made from elderberries or plums or whatever, are unexciting drinking compared with the precious products of the vineyards.

I admit there have been occasional exceptions. I came across

61

one some years ago in a remote village where I happened to be staying, and where, through the chance offer of hospitality to a stranger, I found myself a guest at a festive gathering of the local Methodists. The refreshment which we all consumed, most liberally, was a sparkling white wine made from elderflowers. The Methodists, in the ordinary course of events, were unbending teetotallers and would never bring themselves to enter the local pub for a pint of beer. I think they believed, or chose to believe, that the elderflower wine, being the product of their own virtuous farm kitchens, was non-alcoholic or so nearly so as not to matter; but they were profoundly mistaken. The evening passed in a merry blur. (Surely, I have sometimes wondered subsequently, surely no one laced the drinks with something stronger?) I viewed my hosts, delightful people but hitherto seemingly staid, in a different light thereafter.

It is sad that home-made wine does not often attain such heights; such a fruit as the elderberry, when it hangs in thick purple bunches from every hedge, appears to be meant by nature for this noble purpose. We did once try to follow nature's apparent intentions in this respect, and the elderberries certainly imparted a beautiful and impressive colour to the wine, but unfortunately that seemed to exhaust their capabilities. Those who know better tell us the fault was ours, and I am sure they are right, but the experience was discouraging nevertheless.

There is one traditional and foolproof tipple which we do produce with unfailing success and to the applause of all who are permitted to sample it. This is sloe gin. The virtue of this drink, apart from its delectable character, is that its manufacture is simplicity itself, calling for nor e of the fidgety techniques and nice judgments of wine-making. All you need is a heap of sloes and a bottle of gin, with a little brown sugar. You pierce the skins of the sloes and drop them into the gin, with the sugar; then you leave well alone for three months. If you make it when the sloes are ready to be picked from the hedgerows in the autumn, it will have brought itself to perfection in time to grace your Christmas dinner. Picking the sloes is a pleasant occupation on a sunny autumnal afternoon, especially if you remember where the blackthorn blossom was thickest in the very early days of spring, before even the hawthorns had come into flower. The dark, purple-black fruits are not easy to see at first glance. It is possible to stare into a thicket for several minutes without spotting a single sloe. Then one of them seems to materialise on a branch, and then another, and gradually you come to see them scattered about the bush. Once in a while there is a heavy crop and then there is no difficulty, but that seldom happens with us, for some reason. In other places, notably in Wales, I have seen the spiky blackthorn branches weighed down by huge numbers of these sour little fruits.

I trust I shall find enough this year to have sloe gin ready when Christmas Day comes round again. I only wish I had a dozen bottles of that amazing elderflower concoction to dispose of first.

ELEVEN

The pleasures of midsummer rain are undervalued. It is one of the minor consequences of modern man's obsession with sunshine. The obsession itself is perfectly understandable, given that most people live at two removes from the natural world; firstly, indoors, and secondly, indoors in a large city. When their annual period of release arrives, they head for the sunlit south like deprived addicts with urgent cravings to satisfy. In the country, people do not fully share this yearning, for contrary to popular complaint the English climate affords a great deal of sunshine. It tends to be supplied unpredictably and intermittently, but there is plenty of it, provided that you are there to enjoy it when it comes.

Sometimes it can even seem excessive. We have had a long spell of hot and sunny days lately and after a time gratitude for 'wonderful weather' began to wear thin. The English have been too profoundly conditioned by an almost unceasing variety in their climate not to grow restive when one hot day is followed by another, and then another, for weeks on end. Besides, gardens languish, parched, unless people exert themselves frequently with watering-can or hose; the country assumes a dusty, jaded look; and, ungrateful as it may be, minds turn increasingly to the pleasures of soft, refreshing rain.

It came at last the other evening, after the long drought had culminated in a couple of days of thunderous tension in the air. For a time the heavy green foliage of the trees was motionless. There was a sense of impending drama. Then came the catharsis: a sudden movement of every leaf as a wind emerged without warning from the darkening sky, and a clatter of thunder like some colossal fall of masonry in the clouds, and at last we heard the steady, soothing sound of falling rain.

Next morning the world seemed to have been reborn. It was a dazzling, blowy summer morning with a new vividness of colour everywhere, a new fragrance, a new rejuvenating freshness in the air. As I went over the hillside I remembered Constable's saying, that the best lesson on art he ever received was contained in the words, 'Remember, light and shadow never stand still'—surely a quintessentially English, or at any rate northern, maxim for an artist to cherish. The valley was sparkling after the rain, beneath a sky where clouds, sailing across the blue, made intricate variations of shading in the air and on the land. All those precious English painters who learned to find their subjects in our low landscape and huge, ever-changing skies would have warmed to such a scene; all were beneficiaries of our inconstant northern weather, which so seldom bores, and which fills the sky with infinite variety.

One must be bred in these latitudes, I suppose, to understand. I recall once sitting in an Italian garden in the springtime and remarking with admiration upon the dissolving patterns of brilliant white clouds overhead. My Florentine host gave me a look of disbelief, not to say disgust. To him, the only good sky was one of unsullied blue; the shifting clouds were no more than blemishes, like warts on a beautiful face. There was a gulf between our responses which was unbridgeable, his formed in the bright clarity of Mediterranean light, mine shaped under the endlessly varying ceiling of the north.

The nature of that gulf makes me wonder, sometimes, about the part played by landscape and climate in the forming of that vague concept called 'national character'. Impossible to believe that this context of light and shade, changing without pause, has not impressed itself in some way upon the English mind and emotions, together with the cool green luxuriance of the English rural scene: impossible, too, without descending to the feebly unscientific, to specify what that impress amounts to. One may retreat into sonorous generalisations, as Aldous Huxley did, when, after transplanting himself to Italy, he decided that the north developed the soul, while the south was fruitful of beauty. Yet England was, until we spoiled so much of it, a country of surpassing beauty, as all those poets and writers who 'babbled of green fields' through the centuries have testified. When I try to guess the effect of England upon its people, I am tempted to see the land and its climate as the nursemaids both of a particular kind of individuality and of a distinctive perceptiveness about the natural world; which suggests a notional Englishman who is half Laurence Sterne, half William Wordsworth; and I do not think that is quite as fanciful as might at first appear.

TWELVE

The air is loud with the sounds of the combine harvesters, droning across every hillside. The country has been taken over by an invincible mechanised army. Monstrous machines trundle along narrow lanes, forcing every passer-by to move respectfully aside on to grassy banks; they chew their way inexorably across one ripe field after another. Their untiring advance has subjugated the entire landscape.

Not long ago the combines still seemed strange and mysterious invaders at harvest time. Today, although old men in village pubs continue to exchange memories of times when harvesting was infinitely more laborious and uncertain, these machines have settled into the pattern of life. When, as will surely happen one day, they are superseded by some new technological marvel, we will look back at them with a touch of sentiment, remembering with affection their busy hum and the dry scent of grain which lingers in the warm air as they work. For the present, they are the everyday instruments of the harvesting, which is the climax of the year.

It is a cheerful time and a satisfying time. One remembers at this season that, in spite of all temptations in the other direction which the world sedulously fosters, man retains an instinct towards a certain frugality, a thrifty setting aside of something against the future. The gathering and storing of the crop is agreeable to this primitive need. Much of the sweat and hazard which gave the harvest of former days its drama have gone; the satisfaction in the achievement remains, and is shared by almost everyone in the countryside, whether directly involved or not.

I met an old, retired farmer out in the fields today. Like me, he had gone for the pleasure of the scene, and we watched the stiff-stalked wheat being swept from the ground by the machine. He gave me his verdict on the crop as we strolled across the stubble. I noticed that he was carrying a piece of rusty metal, which, he told me, he had just picked up in a hedge-bottom; it had come off a tractor or a plough, and had lain forgotten in the nettles until his sharp eye spotted it. It did not look much of a trophy to me, and I said something of the sort, wondering what use such a bit of scrap could be to him. The old man was mildly shocked. 'Why,' he said, 'you never know when a bit of iron like that will come in useful.' Then I remembered that his garden shed was stocked with an almost surrealist assortment of such discarded items, old horseshoes, rusty nails, fragments of tools, and much more of that sort, all of which he had picked up in the fields and frugally carried home in case they proved 'useful'. He has the true countryman's squirrel habit.

It is a kind of harvest. He no longer has to work in the fields to bring in the crop, but the inbred impulse of the husbandman still prompts him. 'Waste not, want not'—even though his only crop on this day was a dubiously useful bit of metal. I am not sure where he and his like, with their native thriftiness, belong in a world which makes a virtue of expendability and planned waste. It may be that in the leaner years of the future they will have something to teach the rest; or perhaps the ancient urge towards thrift will not survive in the countryside which is to come. It has persisted so far, however, making one of the clear differences between the countryman and his fellow-worker in the city; and I fancy that as long as country people have to nourish and then harvest their crops, and later to care for them

68

in store, they will never quite succumb to the voices which, unceasingly, try to tempt them into extravagance and waste.

The harvest does not last long now. The whole countryside used to quicken to a breathless *accelerando* of activity; life was charged with excitement, effort and uncertainty; and when the harvest was over the community celebrated with feasting and drinking. In the pattern of modern farming it is not much more than a revving-up of the engine, an extra pressure on the throttle.

No one who has to do the labour of farming pines for the long days of sweat which the machines have freed them from. There are regrets, though, that the fun which used to follow the old, hard harvesting has all but vanished along with the grinding work. It has not entirely vanished. In some villages here they still have an annual 'harvest home' supper to round off the year's work on the land, and jovial gatherings they are, distinguished by the consumption on a manly scale of draught beer and steak-and-kidney puddings. They take their place in a succession which stretches back to remotest antiquity. This was the Old Testament injunction:

'Thou shalt observe the feast of the tabernacles seven days, after that thou hast gathered in thy corn and thy wine. And thou shalt rejoice in thy feast, thou, and thy son, and thy daughter and thy manservant, and thy maidservant, and the Levite, the stranger, the fatherless, and the widow that are within thy gates.'

All these persons, perhaps excepting the Levite, unless the parson took his place, were present at the old harvest feasts, although it was often the custom for the women to withdraw prudently to another place half-way through the evening, when the home-brewed beer was beginning to show its strength. Even the absent stranger had his part to play, since the workers in the fields often enjoyed by local tradition the right to solicit money from any passer-by, as a contribution towards the cost of the coming feast.

The rapidity of the modern harvest has upset some of our habits. People still speak of the 'harvest moon' when they mean the full moon which rises at sunset near the autumnal equinox, but by the time the equinoctial moment arrives the harvest is a

69

thing of the past. The harvest festival service takes place in our village church, by custom, in October, when the sturdy rendering of 'All is safely gathered in' is more a reference to historical fact than a thank-offering by men fresh from the fields. Not that the harvest festival service is itself of great antiquity, although it fits so well with other old harvest customs; it was the invention of a parson in Dorset not much more than a century ago. Today I think that, unintentionally, the burning of the straw after the combines have done their work has slipped into a high place among the secular celebrations. A bonfire is always tinged with ritual, and what began as a utilitarian act of disposal has turned, to some degree, into a celebration and a rite.

For a time, though, the fields of stubble stretch out enticingly in the golden light. Tranquillity settles upon the valley after the bustle of harvesting. I love these fields best of all in the evening, when the low sun dims to a glowing red disc in a shimmering haze, and the landscape rolls gently away into a misty distance where a strip of woodland is as even as a water-colourist's wash of dark green, and the hills beyond that are scarcely more than hints of shape and colour.

There is a sudden opening up of the country, a new richness of space. Instead of picking my way along footpaths I find myself with new tracts of land at my disposal, land lately monopolised by the wheat and barley. The sound of the stubble underfoot is cheerful; it crunches like snow. Where the farmer has baled his straw and stacked it in odd, haphazard groupings, as if in a droll attempt at sculpture, the temptation to follow a random course across the crisp acres is irresistible. This evening I was escorted by swallows and martins, who evidently felt the same urge to tack and zig-zag over the shorn fields. There was a coolness in the air and they must have begun to sense the tug of the south. They swooped and circled almost at ground level, and one could pretend they were having a last playful fling in their summer territory before departing. The pheasants were out in force, clucking and strutting about the stubble. Young pheasants loitered almost until I had trodden on them before they scuttled to cover, showing more indignation than alarm; and they, no less than the swallows, would have to learn new ways before long.

Here and there I found a tiny oak tree, only an inch or two

tall, which had sprung from a scattered acorn under the shelter of the corn. These oak seedlings appear every year and I see their first green leaves catching the autumn sunshine in the stubble. Then they are done for, by fire or by the plough. But the ancient forests of England never give up the struggle to re-assert themselves. This land has been cleared and under the mastery of men for upwards of a thousand years, yet every year the forest, patient and unconquered, tries to return to its old dominion. The present cultivators of these fields, with the armoury of modern agriculture at their command, feel no threat from the incessant, almost secret pressure of the old vegetation; they are far from that narrowly balanced struggle which their earliest predecessors lived through, when the greenwood pressed hard and openly upon their newly acquired fields; but the pressure is still there. It belongs to that unending contest between man and his surroundings out of which this landscape has been formed. When I think of the power which men now invoke in this contest, of the ferocity with which fire is now employed, I find it good that the old adversary can still put up a fight. A farmer gathers his harvest and soon afterwards turns the stubble into a sea of flame; yet the oak-trees reappear each year.

It is wise to make the most of the stubble fields while they are there to be enjoyed, because they do not survive for long. Many people have misgivings about the liberal use of fire to prepare them for the plough. I share these doubts, and yet the burning of the straw is established now as a part of the sequence; and, to be truthful, if often supplies an otherwise absent element of excitement in the modern harvest routine.

I remember an evening in Norfolk not long ago, on that coastline where the sleek countryside, with its woods and fields and stout flint-and-brick farms, reaches to the sea, and the prosperous land yields abruptly to salt marshes and sand dunes. It is a meeting of two worlds. You can stand at the edge of a wheat field and, looking inland, see the combine trundling to and fro and, beyond it, the billowing farmland studded with trees. Turn your back on this, and a wholly different scene begins at your feet: an expanse of flowery marsh, veined with water-courses and a tidal creek, and further off a line of sand dunes, and at last the sea, a strip of indigo upon the horizon.

Two separate systems of life meet there, at a visible frontier. In one direction, all the vegetation and wild life of the fields, in the other the lonely stretches of sea-lavender and marram grass, samphire and sea-holly. Lapwings and pheasants haunt the inland zone. Oyster-catchers and terns and gulls possess the marshes and dunes.

On that evening I walked across the marsh from the seashore and it was an hour of rare calm: not a breath of wind, not a stirring of the air beneath a cloudless sky. Looking towards the land, I saw that a vast pillar of smoke had risen above the corn-fields, reaching up to an almost unbelievable height in the still air, an extraordinary ascending cloud of purple and ochre and earthy red. What horror such a sight would have caused earlier generations of men in that remote place! Once it might have meant that the Danes had landed and gone on their pillaging; later it would have told of some terrible catastrophe to farm or village. On that gentle evening it meant merely that the harvesters had begun to burn the acres of straw left behind by the combines, and that the warm sunshine and the still atmosphere had turned their efforts into a startling spectacle.

Before I had got off the marsh I could smell the smoke, and in the village there was a blue haze. The flames could be seen and heard, leaping and crackling across the hillsides, in furious celebration of the harvest of the machines. When seen at close quarters a well-managed 'burn' in a big field can be exhilarating and, in a slightly shameful way, satisfying. There is a dramatic completeness in the sequence of events, the slow, meticulously careful preparations leading up to the swift and spectacular climax. It appeals to old memories of November the Fifth bonfires, and the gradual accumulation of fuel ending in a happy orgy of destruction. Fire has its allure for the most virtuous of men. There is a little of the arsonist in all of us.

A farmer neighbour mentioned the other day that he was about to burn some sixty acres of wheat straw and I found myself almost without premeditation strolling in his direction at the right moment. It was a hot, dry afternoon and the hillside seemed parched and dusty. The preparations were well advanced. Some people are notoriously careless when they burn their straw, leaving a waste of ruined trees and hedges, but this

72

man is not of that sort. A wide strip of earth had been ploughed round the perimeter of the field, and an inner strip minced up by the rotary-cultivator, to make doubly sure that the fire-break would be effective. Within these barriers, the straw had been laid out for burning, in long parallel rows running the length of the field within a continuous wall of straw.

When all was ready the farmer positioned himself on the windward side and the men stood near him, watching. The golden acres stretched out before them and there was a moment of what seemed, at least, to be hushed solemnity. I thought of the months of ploughing, and seeding, and spraying, and harvesting, that had led up to this; snow, frost, rain, drought, storms and sunshine had all played their part; now came the finish. The farmer took out his box of matches, struck one match only, and dropped it on the first line of straw.

Flames sprang up at once. Two men who had been standing by with pitchforks leaped at the blazing patch and seized forkfuls of burning straw. They ran down the row with these, dropping fire as they went. Then they stood still like the rest of us and watched. The sight was familiar enough, yet I would swear that every man was awed, even a little frightened, by the panic speed with which the fire sped along the rows of straw. Then came the noise. A deep, crackling roar arose, filled with fear and danger. The smoke billowed upwards and moved slowly away in the light breeze.

Within minutes, scarcely a wisp of straw remained. The solitary match-flame had consumed sixty acres. After a time the men went across the blackened field to beat out any lingering islands of flame, men in a festive and light-hearted mood, celebrating the harvest, their mastery of fire, their lordship over the earth. I wondered how many infant oak trees had been turned to ashes. The tang of smoke hung about us as we went back to the village, and although all was still and quiet again, I could imagine the ferocious, implacable roar of the flames echoing faintly from the charred hillside.

THIRTEEN

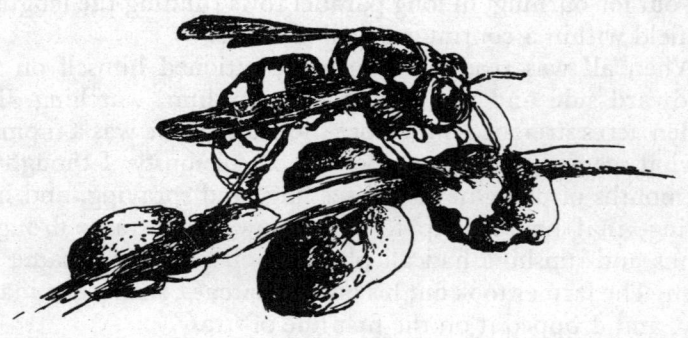

Not for the first time, I find myself at odds with the wisdom of the ages as it has been distilled into proverbial form. It is better, we are told, to be stung by a nettle than pricked by a rose. In its figurative meaning, that it is less hurtful to be wronged by an enemy than by a friend, perhaps so; but I am frequently pricked by the thorns of my roses and think nothing of it, whereas when I was caught unawares by a nettle today and given a thorough sting on the back of my hand, the irritation nagged at me for hours.

I suppose it is a sign of the passing years, but I am seldom stung by nettles nowadays. When I was a boy it seemed to be happening all the time. One grows more careful about exposing oneself to such small discomforts. On this occasion I was passing through a wood where hardly anyone goes. I noticed too late that the path had shrunk to the narrowest of defiles, by reason of a belt of lank nettles which had sprung up along the neglected way, sprawling in their usual lackadaisical fashion in all directions. There were no dock-leaves nearby so I could not apply the traditional remedy on the spot, and in any case that is another piece of ancestral wisdom about which I have my doubts. It has come down to us through the centuries, I know; it is vouched for by authorities as far back as Chaucer and possibly farther; but in my experience its merit is unproven. Perhaps I have never mastered the technique, although I can remember staining my skin green with dock-leaves often enough. The treatment never seemed to have much effect.

There is this to be said for nettles—they die away early in the season and leave the field clear for the clumsiest of pedestrians. Already, I noticed, the colour was draining away from the leaves, giving them the distinction of being the first growing things to signal the approach of autumn in this way. Quite soon they will wither. But as examples of evolution they puzzle me (as, I regret to say, evolution so often does). That nettles are soft and juicy inside their formidable defences, and so would doubtless be eaten in large quantities if they did not protect themselves with drops of poison, is obvious enough; in fact they are still gathered and eaten by some people, even though far removed from the modern category of 'convenience foods'. But then, many other plants are also good to eat and are in fact eaten: by what process did the nettle decide that it alone would have no more of this, but would develop its armature of poisonous hairs to discourage the eaters? It is, I am sure, a foolish question, no more sensible than childish inquiries about the 'use' of un-attractive creatures such as slugs. But then, why did some other plants, the dead-nettle for example, develop so as to seek safety in merely *imitating* the nettle's forbidding appearance, instead of acquiring their own defences? I suppose I should know better than to ask myself such questions.

At least I could reflect consolingly upon the benevolence of the English countryside, which hardly ever offers any greater threat than this trifling itch from a nettle-sting. Years ago, I went from New York to spend a peaceful weekend with friends on Long Island, and was greeted by a host whose arm was hidden in a massive cocoon of bandages from wrist to shoulder. 'Poison ivy,' he said, brusquely, when I asked what dreadful accident had happened to him. Now that is a truly hostile form of vege-tation. Not as fearsome, perhaps, as the famous Burning Nettle (or Devil's Leaf) of Java, which is said to kill its victims on occasion, or to cause terrible pain for months; but still, bad enough. We are really fortunate in our nettles. The same is true of wild creatures in these islands. Very infrequently someone is bitten by an adder, but generally speaking there is no living creature which offers any serious threat to man. With us, nature has been tamed. The worst that most people encounter in their lifetime is the sting of a wasp, and while that can be painful and unpleasant it is nothing compared with what one has to guard against elsewhere.

Wasps, as it happens, seem to be abnormally plentiful this year. I say 'seem to be' because I half-suspect we make the same observation in most years; it does sometimes happen that the numbers are plainly below or above average, but usually I think the fact is that the life-cycle of the wasp, with its secret build-up of numbers and its sudden show of strength towards the end of the season, retains its power to take us by surprise. Except in the case of those unfortunate people with an irrational dread of spiders, wasps must be the most unpopular of all common creatures. There is something unsettling about the low drone they make in flight, and their black and yellow uniform looks hostile and fierce, especially to anyone who has felt the burning pain of their sting. Possibly the chief thing to be said in their favour (from a human point of view) is that they are unlikely to make use of their armament unless they feel themselves to be under attack. The trouble with this as a basis for peaceful co-existence is that if one of them should be sat upon or bitten or otherwise accidentally threatened, it will not pause to consider the motives of its assailant before counter-attacking. Still, it is something.

Nevertheless we do our best to destroy any wasps' nests near the house. I find it surprisingly hard to track wasps to their lair; it can be done by patient observation, but it takes time. The only short-cut I have heard recommended does not greatly appeal to me. It involves tying a long, white thread around a wasp's waist and then watching it travel back to base, much slowed and much more visible as a result of this treatment. I dare say it works well enough, for anyone who is willing to take on the job of harnessing a wasp.

The nests usually turn out to be in holes in the ground, although I have come across them inside buildings and in rotten tree-stumps. Once we were afflicted by one in our roof, and when it was taken out the following winter it proved to be more than two feet in diameter. They are, as a matter of fact, rather marvellous constructions, made more impressive by the know-ledge that each of these intricate, beautifully built colonies is the work of one short summer. If wasps could make honey, as bees do, they could prolong the life of their communities beyond a season; lacking that talent, the species puts the task of re-creating social life upon each queen when she emerges in spring from solitary hibernation. Sometimes early in the year I find the small nests which the queens build to found their communities; one appeared just above our front door, a neat construction about the size of a hen's egg, made out of paper manufactured from tiny scrapings of wood pulped with the queen's saliva. The queen lays an egg in each of the cells she builds. When the eggs hatch she hunts for food (flies, caterpillars and suchlike creatures) for the larvae; when the first wasps emerge, she lets others take over the work of extending the nest and foraging, and devotes herself to more egg-laying—with the result that by the end of the summer she is probably reigning over many thousands of wasps, a rate of multiplication which it would be hard to credit were it not for the annual mass invasion which it leads to.

Remarkable though this performance is, it is hard to look kindly upon a wasp. An instinct for self-protection supervenes. I know only one record of an allegedly affectionate relationship between a man and a wasp—that left by Sir John Lubbock, an eminent Victorian scientist, politician and social reformer (who was responsible for the introduction of Bank Holidays, among other enlightened measures). He kept a pet wasp for nine months, taking her from her nest in May when she had laid eggs in some twenty cells but before any of these had hatched, so that she was, as he benignly noted, 'as yet alone in the world'.

I enjoy the good Sir John's account of his friendship as it appears in his almost-forgotten work, *Ants, Bees and Wasps*. She was 'shy and nervous' at first and 'kept her sting in constant readiness'. In the early days she stung him once or twice—'I think, however, entirely from fright'. Later she became so used to him that she seemed to enjoy being stroked and fed happily from his hand, and for months he never even caught sight of her sting, let alone felt it.

His narrative of her last days is an affecting piece of Victorian sentiment blended with nice observation.

'When cold weather came on she fell into a drowsy state and I began to hope she would hibernate and survive the winter. I kept her in a dark place but watched her carefully and fed her if ever she seemed at all restless.

'She came out occasionally and seemed as well as usual until near the end of February, when one day I observed she had nearly lost the use of her antennae, although the rest of her body was as usual. She would take no food. Next day I tried again to feed her; but the head seemed dead, though she could still move her legs, wings and abdomen. The following day I offered her food for the last time; but both head and thorax were dead and paralysed; she could but move her tail—a last token, as I could almost fancy, of gratitude and affection. As far as I could judge, her death was quite painless.'

Perhaps it troubled Sir John to know how he could fittingly dispose of the corpse, but he solved the problem in characteristic style. He said farewell to his friend and donated her remains to the British Museum.

FOURTEEN

Uninvited, I helped myself to an apple from a bough bent low over a hedge in the village. The weight of the fruit held it down temptingly at shoulder height, it was a good, sharp apple although I could not put a name to it, and it seemed the sensible thing to do. Even if the rightful owner were watching me through his windows he would have had no reason to complain (not that I could altogether stifle the hope that he was doing no such thing). There are more than enough apples for everyone. Sometimes I read that professional growers are bothered by over-production, but there are no professionals in this parish. We gather our apples and pears for our own pleasure and thereby remain happily free from the stresses of economics, holding, as our distant predecessors must have done in their struggle to feed themselves from this patch of earth, that a glut is the best of all crops.

I have in an outbuilding a wooden construction, rather like a primitive chest of drawers built on a grand scale, which has stored the apples of more autumns than I have lived through; it is already full to the brim. In the garden a musty fragrance arises from the fallen fruit as it ferments in the wet grass, attacked by wasps who burrow gluttonously into the flesh. Out in the hedges the wild crab-apples have been equally abundant, spreading a fruity quagmire over the ground. At such a time no orchard-owner could begrudge the odd apple to a passer-by. People who do not own fruit trees, in fact, find themselves repeatedly pressed to fill baskets from orchards which have produced more fruit than can be stored. This takes all meaning out of the old pursuit of 'scrumping', as the disreputable but seductive practice of raiding orchards used to be called in my boyhood, and there is now nothing like the old zest for illicit apple-picking. Time was when it was part of the cycle of the seasons for village boys, like bird's-nesting or collecting conkers; a fruit-grower had to keep constant watch if he wished to enjoy the whole of his crop, and the police were sometimes called in to discourage the more ambitious raiders. Like old-fashioned poaching, the practice has all but died away along with the social conditions which produced it. If modern country boys feel the pangs of untimely hunger they are more likely to spend money on sweets in the village shop than to rob someone else's apple-trees.

In hungrier days, fruit-stealing was not confined to boys, any more than poaching. The advice which William Cobbett gave on laying out a fruit garden, in his *English Gardener*, says much about rural life of the times, for he planned an orchard like a fortress, alotting an astonishing amount of space to a system of defences against thieves. To begin with he stipulated a high wall; outside that were to be, firstly, a dense and thorny hedge and, beyond that, a ditch six feet deep. This from Cobbett, the passionate friend of England's starveling and dispossessed peasantry! He confessed to feeling remorse 'in plotting thus against the poor fellows', but he saw no other course if the crop was to be saved. The owner of an orchard had to take the threat of robbery as seriously as any rich man of today safeguarding his jewellery and his silver.

The rise in prosperity which has dispelled the spectre of that hungry army, waiting to invade any orchard whose defences it could overcome, may perhaps account also for the present national indifference to the gastronomic riches offered by English apple-trees. This is the country in which apples reach perfection, and many a piece of England is to the apple what the Côte d'Or is to the grape, yet this delicious piece of good fortune is held in low esteem. How many shops keep a respectable selection of our beautiful apples, and how many people would buy them if they did? A good apple at its best, a Cox's Orange Pippin, say, or a golden-yellow Egremont Russet, is more to be prized than any exotic fruit you care to name; it presents the palate with a wonderfully effervescent, aromatic complexity of flavour and texture; yet it does not receive its due. I have noticed that men with an informed appreciation of apples usually have similarly good taste in wine. The two pleasures go happily together, and I suspect a certain significance in the fact that the great Mr Cox, who bred his magnificent Orange Pippin in 1830, was a brewer, in an age when the brewing of beer was more akin to art than to chemistry. Benefactor of mankind as he was, if poor Cox's name had not happened to be attached to that of his masterpiece, by now he would have been all but lost to history, even though he gave us the finest apple in the world.

'Comfort me with apples,' says the Song of Solomon in a phrase which stirs the mind like a vision of bliss for all right-thinking fruit-munchers; but that, too, is no longer in favour and is, if the scholars of the New English Bible are to be believed, nothing but a translator's blunder. 'He refreshed me with raisins' is the preferred reading now. 'Comfort me with apples' sounds infinitely more alluring than any paltry offer of raisins. It suggests that our forebears were right about fruit even if fallible in handling ancient texts. When I inspect my loaded apple-rack, I am filled with a sense of comforts in store against the future.

Apart from bringing increased respect for other people's orchards, greater affluence has also caused a loss of interest in the free gifts which the countryside offers at this time of year. Hazel-nuts, crab-apples, wild plums, sloes—almost everything is left to the birds and the squirrels. To be accurate, the squirrels in this part of England do not leave us much choice so far as nuts are concerned. Other fruits, however, are there for the picking. Few people think it worth the trouble.

The blackberry is the exception. There are enough of these to meet all demands, of course, and this year the supply is vast; all the same I have been impressed by the zeal with which some people in the village set about gathering them. There are a few places, notably at the disused gravel pit which has become a wilderness, where the blackberries grow large and luscious and, what is important to the gatherer, in comfortably accessible situations. More than once I have passed that way lately and noticed that the entire crop of fully ripened fruit had been removed from all the more convenient places. At first this was puzzling. I enjoy blackberries and I acknowledge that no apple-pie can be brought to perfection without them, to counterpoint the apple flavours; but still, a few blackberries go a long way. It was not until I came across two ladies of the village filling huge plastic bags, and doing so in a lively competitive spirit, that the explanation was made plain to me. They were gathering fruit in bulk for their deep-freezers. This adds a new dimension to the ancient autumn practice of harvesting the hedges and wild places.

The birds are unchanging and ruthless in their attacks upon the fruit gardens. Not growing soft fruits myself on a scale to justify one of those cages of netting which function like inverted aviaries, keeping the birds outside and the fruit within, I resign myself to losing most of what I do grow, particularly since our cat grew too old and lethargic to patrol the garden with her natural ferocity. On the whole I think it a fair exchange. Spring would be unthinkable without birds singing in every tree and I enjoy their presence all through the year; even the gardener in me is gratified when I see a thrush gorging on my surplus of snails, breaking each shell with a blow on a large flint which serves as his anvil; or when I watch a bluetit tirelessly carrying green caterpillars to its nest to feed its young. It is only when they steal my fruit too brazenly that I feel my hospitality wearing thin.

Mostly I grieve over the unrelenting way in which the birds raid the gooseberries. I happen to possess a couple of admirable old gooseberry bushes in one corner of my garden. I call them admirable not only because of their dignified appearance but also out of respect for their old age and their prolific production of large, juicy and delectable fruit. I have no idea what variety of gooseberry these are, or even whether it still exists officially; what I do know is that I look forward each year to savouring the delicious berries. So, I sometimes think, do the blackbirds. They attack without restraint, often without troubling to wait until the fruit has ripened. I take a certain morbid interest in the spectacle. The bushes are, of course, spiky and inhospitable to any bird which wishes to alight there, but the blackbirds are indifferent to that. They swoop upon the bushes, banging and shaking the branches with their wings, administering blows with their beaks, and making such a commotion that if they fail to grab a gooseberry straight from the bush some of the ripest fruits invariably fall to the ground to be seized and eaten. It is a melancholy sight for a gooseberry-fancier, made the more so by the turpitude of the old cat, who lies on the lawn in the sun watching with shameful unconcern.

They usually leave me a little of the fruit, however, which I eat straight from the bush. A friend from Paris once ate two or three in this way and exclaimed indignantly, 'Why cannot I buy such fruit in France?' I could not explain the French neglect of the gooseberry. It is one of the mysteries of their gastronomy. I could only press him to eat some more, before the birds finished them off.

FIFTEEN

Yesterday the pheasants were lording it over the fields, the sun catching a rainbow brilliance on their plumage. I came across a dozen of them strutting about a green pasture—a classic English rural scene although a paradoxical one, for pheasants are not only exotic but are patently so. After many centuries they still look outlandish, different, flashily foreign: and yet they belong. They paraded around with a proprietorial air.

Today there is no sun and the sound of gunfire is heard from the hillside. Landrovers are parked on the stubble and the shooters are at work, mostly men who come here for the day to enjoy the sport they have paid for. I met the keeper during the morning and he said they were doing pretty well, and I was glad more for his sake than for that of the men with the guns.

Like the old village poachers, the gamekeepers are a shrunken fraternity. They linger on rather as isolated garrisons left behind by an army; often somewhat solitary men, in place of the squads of keepers and under-keepers who prepared the sport of the Victorian and Edwardian rich. Last year a shower of spent pellets rattled the hedge near me as I was walking along a footpath when the guns were out, and the keeper was quick to come up with apologies and excuses. His forebears, I fancy, would have adopted a more cavalier attitude towards such trifles as public rights of way. Only the pheasants are as arrogant as of old, when they are safely showing off their oriental plumage in the autumn sun, before the panic days of the guns.

The keepers whose lives have changed least must, I imagine, be those who look after the grouse moors. I have an old friend who has spent his life caring for a remote and rugged stretch of Yorkshire moor, and whenever possible I like to visit him in his hillside cottage during the shooting season. For me it is welcome news when the grouse season is a good one; I love the places where the sport takes place, and so have a concern for their prosperity, but also I know what it means to my friend Tom. If the birds are plentiful and healthy I find him in excellent spirits when I get to the end of the long, rough track which leads to his cottage; if they are scarce, as a result of unfriendly weather or disease, he is downcast.

There are not many men left in England today who live in such isolation as he and his wife. Their small stone cottage stands almost at the head of a dale, facing a superb prospect of steep-sided glacial valley flanked by rounded uplands tinted purple-brown by the heather. The only neighbours occupy a farmhouse so far below that my friend sees more of their slate roof than he ever sees of them. He has never bothered with the extravagance of a telephone, and even if he had, the winter snowstorms would probably put it out of action. When he goes out of his door it is usually to go upwards, towards the moors and even further from human society, rather than downwards, into the more sociable valley. It would be wildly wrong, however, to picture Tom and his wife as a pair of depressed recluses made gloomy by their lonely lives. On the contrary, they are a most inspiriting couple to call on. They exude a cheerful resilience and their hospitality is of an unaffected, instantaneous kind which seems curiously archaic. It is the hospitality of people to whom a friendly visit is a surprise and an event. The kettle is set on the fire which blazes in the kitchen every day of the year, the tins of home-made cakes and home-made ginger biscuits are produced, chairs are arranged round the hearth, and the affairs of the dale are passed under lively, often hilarious, review. I suppose, although to say as much to them would be a fearful gaffe, that their cottage interior could be transported in its entirety to some museum of

85

rural life, where it would be admired for its antique snugness. The stone floor is partly covered by rag rugs which Tom's wife has made. There is a wooden dresser; the wooden chairs are padded with comfortably worn cushions; on the white-washed walls are a couple of dim pictures of moorland shooting scenes and a primitive old glass barometer, of dubious reliability. Yet there is no impression of tiresome quaintness on the visitor from the outside world. Quite the opposite: one is caught up in a jolly bustle and at once forgets that here is a survival of an older pattern of English life, because in this secluded place it is still the natural order. I feel gratitude that our small and overcrowded island can still, if only in odd corners, find room for a way of living so deeply at variance with the habits of the urban herd.

Notwithstanding the sound of the guns, with its intimations of mortality, the arrival of autumn has brought a cheerful stir into our softer southern valley. It is an excellent time of year to get about the country on one's legs. No less than those first, seductive days of spring, these restless, changeable autumnal days pull at one to be out and about. The year seems to be spinning the wheel at random before the final collapse into winter. One day the whirling winds throw left-over bits of summer across the valley, all blue sky and warm air; then an early fragment of winter arrives, chilly and grey; later a mild calm settles over the land.

The windy days are the most intrusive. From my window in the morning I watch the rooks tumbling in the gusty air above their nests, and they make me itch to be out of doors. I owe a debt of gratitude to the rooks, gratitude for the hours of agreeable ambling around the parish they have led me to when I might have been more dutifully employed. They are not alone in their rush of autumnal high spirits. When I had walked through their wood to the hilltop fields, escorted on the way by much boisterous cawing, I came across a huge congregation of plover, and they too seemed to have endless energy to spare. Long before I was near enough to justify alarm they rose from the ground, one or two at first, followed by a gathering throng until the whole multitude, many hundreds strong, was in the air. While I skirted their field, for perhaps fifteen or twenty minutes, the cloud of birds remained overhead; each member was performing spirited aerobatics as if in fully independent flight and yet the whole flock stayed bound together by I know not what means of communication. Looking back later, I saw them drop back to earth with the same unanimity. Perhaps I should have felt compunction at having taken up half an hour of their time, but they made so elaborate an aerial display out of it that they might have been grateful for the excuse.

During the patches of sunshine the bright fruits seemed to glow in the hedges. Busy packs of small birds bustled along the branches. All the hedgerows were festooned with that feathery clematis called 'Traveller's Joy', so named presumably because it adorns the wayside to the pleasure of a travelling man, most aptly at this season which tempts people out of doors. As I walked beside one rambling, overgrown hedgerow I remembered visiting a garden recently in which I was invited to admire the 'tapestry hedge' which was being created. By dint of complicated planting arrangements and well-planned juxtapositions, the owner was achieving a pleasing pattern of foliage, but the effect was dimmer and duller than that produced by this wild bank of trees and shrubs.

It contained a good assortment of different species, which usually means that there has been a hedge on the site for a great many years. Professor W. G. Hoskins, in the course of his investigations into local history, evolved the theory that for every hundred years of its life in an unmanaged condition, a hedge-bank will have added one more species of shrub to its flora. This may seem a surprisingly slow rate of addition; but there are hedges which have served as boundaries for a thousand years or more without interruption. Where a hedge-bank forms a boundary of a parish, or of a farmstead which is recorded in the Domesday Book, it may possibly date from Saxon times.

The hedge I was examining disclosed ten different species, to a casual count. Once, as I could see, it had been two parallel hedges, separated by a narrow track, but they had been allowed to grow together as the track fell out of use. I looked it up on the Ordnance map later and found that it was, as I had suspected, the parish boundary. It has a long history behind it, for all its neglected state nowadays. Other such tracks have grown more important with the passing of time, ending up in our day as metalled roads; this one has dwindled into disuse. But the hedge is still there, marking the limit of the parish and lighting up the autumn fields with its many-coloured leaves and berries.

There were two or three pollarded trees, of great age, in the hedge. It was often the custom, in the days when all fuel had to be found locally, for a few such trees to be left as a perquisite for the farm workers, from which they could cut themselves logs each winter. Perhaps these had once served that purpose, although they are lost in senility now and produce scarcely any new growth. Ivy has taken them over, softening the gnarled outlines of the ancient boles.

Unlike most other things in the autumnal scene, the ivy was still in full flower, holding up dense clusters of fluffy yellow-green to the light. Ever since I was rid of the popular fallacy that ivy strangles trees, I have enjoyed its presence without reservation, and on these late days it is at its best, suddenly producing an almost frivolous froth of flower in contrast with its normal sombreness. There is something strange about its way of growth, to my mind; the sinuous, climbing tendrils are only the first part of the story, although perhaps they are the only part that most people are aware of. Once it has reached the top of its wall, or whatever else it is clinging to, ivy undergoes a change of character. Instead of reaching out ever further with its tendrils, it produces short, stiffer growths, which form what is almost a separate shrub with a rounded head. It is there that the flowers appear. All along the way I saw them soaking up the sunshine.

In one of the woods some distance from the village there is an ivy-covered ruin, an old cottage which has not been habitable for half a century or more, although some of its walls, and most of the brick chimney-stack, still stand precariously. As I drew near its sunlit clearing I heard the steady hum of bees, curiously loud. Then I saw that the ivy which has smothered the tumble-down house was bearing innumerable flowers, and these were quivering beneath a horde of busy bees. The warm air, and the bright sunshine, and the buzzing of the bees, made it seem like a perfect summer's day.

The illusion could not but be brief. The trees are discarding their leaves in a litter of browns and yellows and reds. They announce the passing of time as clearly as the sounding of the church clock in the valley. Sometimes people have found it melancholy that, even on a summer's day, every green leaf is under sentence of early execution. Perhaps it is better to remember that even now, as the dead leaves are falling, the greenery of next spring is already formed in miniature within the bud.

At night the wind blew stronger, sending a shiver down the valley. One day soon, perhaps tomorrow, we shall wake up to winter.

SIXTEEN

A frosty November morning decorates the leafless trees to perfection. When I went up the hill the white hoar was sparkling, and the bare trees arose on all sides like triumphs of architecture, not the lifeless lumps of engineering confected by today's architects but marvellously intricate gothic structures, their soaring vaults and infinite detail all marked out by the frost and lit by the rays of the rising sun. There were layers of milky mist hanging in the air and the calling of the rooks echoed hollowly in the treetops.

The frost has not yet taken to lingering on the trees in the morning. The air was soon mild. When I went to plant a new tree just received from the nursery, a gentle moistness prevailed. As I dug the hole the soil moved easily beneath the spade, soft and damp. Planting a tree is pleasant work, encouraging optimistic thoughts about the future, and especially so when conditions are as favourable as this. The frail roots settle unresistingly into the loam and compost and bone-meal, pressed into the pit that has been dug; and the infant thing, little more than a twig, is magnified in the imagination into a handsome and graceful maturity.

The village has responded readily to the urgings addressed to the country as a whole to plant more trees. In various corners single saplings are being installed; where more space is available, groups are being planted. A decision as to what to plant is not arrived at without much discussion, opinion being split, in general terms, between decorative exotics which put on a great show of blossom and those less meretricious trees, unfortunately slower in growth, which are more traditional to the village scene. To my relief the latter choice has been preferred. My immediate contribution has been to plant on the grassy edge of the lane which passes my house. Since there is no room for anything tall (and nothing is more dismal than seeing a tree outgrow its space and of necessity come under rough surgery), I chose a white hawthorn, and as I set it in the earth I could picture it giving pleasure to people who will walk along this lane many years from now, long after I am dead.

I judge this to be the third occasion during the past few centuries when a significant attempt to enrich the village stock of trees has been made. It is possibly overdue, for although we are generously supplied with magnificently-grown specimens, they are in many cases advancing towards the end of their life-span, so that in perhaps fifty years' time a large number of them must have vanished; and unless we take action now, the impoverishment of the village will be appalling.

A great many of our trees date from the second half of the eighteenth century. Nearly all our horse-chestnuts, for example, are of this vintage. I like to think of the bewigged gentlemen of those days walking about our village in earnest discussion of the art of planting; the village itself cannot have looked very different, except for the absence of such modern introductions as metalled roads, motor-cars, and so forth. Doubtless those people planted chiefly for their own satisfaction but they also served posterity well, and I hope they had some pleasure in the knowledge that succeeding generations would thank them.

The second planting phase seems to have occurred about a hundred years later, in the confident days of the Victorian countryside, and there is a fine assortment of trees today to bear witness to it. To this period, certainly, belong the two Wellingtonias which still dignify the scene. It is never difficult to fix the date of Wellingtonias, because the species was not brought to this country until 1853, and many surviving specimens were planted in the eighteen-sixties, as were ours.

And now, after the passing of another century, we are trying to sustain the tradition. Most of the individual efforts (my own included) have been prompted by a desire to improve the planter's own surroundings as well as to confer a benefit upon the village at large, which seems right and sensible and in keeping with the tradition. The eighteenth-century parson who put a cedar on the rectory lawn was intending, of course, to please himself thereby, but equally he benefited us all. We who are now putting little trees in places where, one day, they will be seen to advantage from our own windows are doing the same. The whole affair is a sane combination of self-interest and thought for the general good.

It was one of the several splendid trees in the old rectory garden which lately gave us all a poignant reminder of the need to plant for the future now, if we were not to dishonour our forebears' good example. Catastrophe threatened a superlative walnut—not the common walnut, which is handsome enough, but the so-called Black Walnut, *Juglans nigra*, which, as this specimen shows, achieves with age a marvellous size and grandeur. Our walnut (we all feel a proprietorial pride in it) has been maturing for upwards of two hundred years and must indeed have been one of the first of its kind to be introduced here from the North American colonies; and in that time it has attained a height and spread which make strangers stop and stare, especially in the spring when its leaflets are a delicate pale green. But not long ago, with a thunderous crash, one of the great branches tore itself free and fell in ruins on the lawn. Soon afterwards another branch split away and plunged down beside the first.

Luckily for all of us the garden is in worthy hands, so the

walnut-tree, instead of being declared unsafe and felled forthwith, was put under the scrutiny of a tree surgeon, who, after an examination, announced that the patient could yet be saved if certain remedial measures were taken. Soon afterwards a gang of his minions appeared. The tree was festooned with ropes and invaded by ladders, presenting us with a scene rather like some large-scale, slow-motion reproduction of a hospital operating theatre. The object was to reduce by one third the overall size of the old tree, removing those portions of branches which the specialist had judged unsafe, and although it was painful to see the ancient limbs being cut, it was also cheering to know that the result would be a healthy future instead of an abrupt end.

The leader of the team was a bearded young man in colourful clothes who gave an impression of perhaps being an actor between engagements. In fact he turned out to be a professional and an enthusiast; he mourned for every bough that was removed, then glowed with pleasure at the thought that it was all in the old tree's best interests. 'Isn't she beautiful?' he asked me, rhetorically, as I stood beside him one day. 'What people forget', he said, 'is that trees have to be cared for when they get on in years, like people. And even then they all have a natural life and have to die at the end of it.' He shook his head mournfully. 'But she'll be good for another hundred years when we've finished.' With that consoling thought we bore the screech of the mechanical saw with fortitude, and, I think, profited from the reminder that mortality will one day claim the most noble of our trees, that we owe a debt to the future in return for the pleasure bequeathed to us by the past.

Had I the means I would indulge without limit in the pleasure of planting. I would rather be rich in trees and woods than in money. I would plant oak and ash and even elm, taking precautions against the hateful elm disease; and beech and hornbeam, lime and horse-chestnut, hawthorn and alder, with silvery willows beside my river and shapely maples on my parkland. Then there would be yews and hollies for seclusion, and a weeping elm to make a bower, and all the fruits for the orchards; and here and there something a little out of the ordinary, such as a mulberry.

I would certainly not omit the mulberry. Some friends of mine are rescuing and replanting an eighteenth-century garden, with agreeable historical associations, which had fallen into ruin. I envy them their opportunity, although much labour is involved. My part has been the unstrenuous one of deciding what to give by way of contribution towards the re-stocking: and it was plain to me that what such a venture emphatically needed was a mulberry, which is the tree associated more than any other with ancient houses and their gardens. Its gnarled appearance fits perfectly into a setting of mellowed antiquity; and since the mulberry is obliging enough to assume this venerable look quite early in its long life, I have hopes of seeing this specimen in its picturesque prime, in reality as well as in imagination.

I wonder that more mulberries are not planted. Apart from the tree's delightful appearance, its fruit is also delicious, with a fine sharp flavour unlike any other. The traditional method of gathering the fruit is to spread cloths upon the ground and then to shake the branches until the berries fall off. These somewhat resemble the raspberry in appearance but botanically they are quite different, and as they ripen they change from a striking red to a rich purple and ultimately they become almost black. Our ancestors, who planted many mulberries, knew what they were about.

Part of the mulberry's attraction, then, derives from its link with gardeners of the distant past. There is a pleasure in experimenting with new products of the plantsman's skill, but at least an equal pleasure in following ancient examples. The mulberry was extensively cultivated by the Greeks and the Romans, and doubtless the Romans brought it here together with many other trees and plants. Perhaps it was lost again in the dark ages after the Romans' departure: like so much that would be of interest in the history of gardening, that information is lacking. What seems reasonably certain is that it was re-introduced in the sixteenth century and planted in a monastery garden at Brentford in Middlesex. There used to be an economic motive for encouraging the culture of mulberries, for the leaves are, of course, the food of the silkworm, and James I imported mulberry trees and seeds with the intention of making the British silk industry independent of foreign supplies. I suppose this commercial incentive greatly encouraged the spread of the tree across the gardens of the country in Stuart times. Seventeenth-century London had a famous place of resort known as 'the Mulberry Garden', which was, so John Evelyn noted in his diary, 'the only place of refreshment about the town for persons of the best quality to be exceedingly cheated at'. This pleasure ground for the worldly occupied part of the site now filled, more decorously, by Buckingham Palace and its gardens.

The mulberry will not, I dare say, recover its lost popularity, but as long as there are gardens there will be other trees of grace and interest grown, to bring those gardens to life. It is away from the places where people live, out in the fields, that the thought that much of England may become a treeless prairie, one day, gains force and sometimes becomes oppressive. Even before the elm disease began its modern ravages, the incompatibility between today's agriculture and trees in hedges had impoverished much of the landscape. It is a dismal prospect which I try not to think about.

What I do see, as I go about this parish, is the abundant evidence of man's intimate dependence upon trees in other times. We are still dependent upon trees, but rather as a source of raw material obtained in bulk from huge commercial forests, which lie across the earth like a suffocating blanket. The relationship used to be more direct, more local and more varied.

Not least, the sportsman left his mark upon the landscape. Those handsome mixed plantings of deciduous trees, established long ago to shelter game or foxes, spinneys which have lately blazed with autumnal colours on the sides of the valley—they would surely not be there, but for the country landowner's ancient passion for killing wild creatures. But what a joy to the eye they provide, when every tree is going down into winter austerity in a last carnival of colour. The unsentimental fact is that most of the trees about us were put there for a utilitarian purpose, or if not put there at least allowed to remain and flourish for such a reason. If the hedgerow trees were not established to provide fuel or shade, then they were usually grown simply to produce timber when their felling-time arrived. The Enclosures, in this as in so much else, were in many places the historic turning-point; the business of enclosing land was a fine thing for the rich but it was costly, and the practice they adopted to recoup some of the expense was to plant their new hedges thickly with trees. One seldom sees nowadays a landscape with hedges as it must have looked in many places after the Enclosures, with the young trees lining the thorn hedges as close to one another as they could be crowded. Often the happy, random scatter of old trees in today's hedges (where they have been allowed to survive at all) is only a faint reminder of the density of planting which once existed.

The old landowners planted what offered the best returns: walnut sometimes, but more often oak, ash or elm. Oak was precious timber but no one could expect to enjoy the profit in his lifetime. 'Three hundred years to grow, three hundred years standing still, and three hundred years dying,' according to the old saying, is the life-cycle of an oak-tree, and although it is ready for felling as timber before its second hundred years are up, it is still too slow for all but the most far-sighted of planters. Ash was also valuable and it is much quicker; but ash starves the land beneath it. Elm produced timber that was much in demand, it grows quickly and easily, and it is tolerant of other vegetation growing at its base; so the richness of elm trees which has come to seem an inseparable part of the English landscape was brought into being.

Some of the old beams in my house are elm, I have been told, not oak as people tend to assume. Elm was used for much more than coffins. Some of the timber in the old wooden ships was elm, its great durability in water being at least as useful there as in the grave. For the same reason it was used for drain-pipes and water-pipes (and even in Victorian England wooden water-pipes were in common use). The wood of the alders, which now grow in neglected profusion beside the ponds in the deserted gravel pit, was also once prized for making pipes which would remain in the wet earth, undecayed, for many years. Alder wood was also the normal material for the soles of clogs, because of those same qualities. Almost every kind of tree had its recognised uses in those days before technology rendered the whole system of crafts and materials obsolete. Ash, because it steamed and bent easily, was for the framework of vehicles. The flexible shoots of willows were for baskets and hurdles. Yew turned easily into bowls (and further back, of course, supplied the wood of the long-bow). Beech was for the furniture-maker. The sweet-chestnut, because it splits easily and resists decay, is to this day a popular fencing material. Hornbeam used to be the usual wood for the teeth of cogs or wooden screws, in which its hardness and strength served well until metal took its place. There were a thousand of these daily applications for the wood of the country-side, almost all of them now superseded.

Yet as I see it we need trees now as much as ever men did, although in a different sense. We may not need timber for all the ingenious practical purposes it used to serve, but we need the trees for refreshment of the eye and of the spirit. A land of cities set in a blank plain may conform to the inhuman dictates of economics: it could never be the home of a sane people. It is possible, I suppose, that in a future age of scarcity men may turn again to many-propertied wood for their daily articles, in grati-tude for a raw material which will reproduce itself for ever; but however that may be, and if we never again need the durable wood of the alder for our clogs, we shall always need trees for our souls.

SEVENTEEN

Something unexpected, and rather disturbing, happened while the valley was gradually settling into winter. We had the first hint of it during the last days of summer, when a spell of dry weather lengthened into a drought. The river seemed to be shrinking more than usual. There was no longer any need to walk to one of the bridges to cross the water. You could scramble down a dry bank, on to a miniature strand of gravel and dusty earth, and then step across the stream as easily as over a garden path.

Ordinarily this would have been put right as soon as autumn came, but when we looked to see the normal healthy flow again, it was not there. The forlorn trickle dwindled even more until, for half a mile of its course, the river vanished entirely. No one could remember anything like it. At the place where, long ago, some village imitator of Capability Brown had dammed the stream to form a lake, there is normally a waterfall splashing over the sluice into a shaded pool, sending the river briskly on its way down the valley. With the lake half-empty there was not a trickle of water, not the merest whisper of a splash, over the mossy stones. Below this point, instead of water there were drifts of dry leaves between the banks, and stones set in a river-bed that had itself turned from mud into something very like stone. The river did not contain water until various ditches had contributed their midget trickles, and even then it revived ingloriously, in a chain of small ponds; only gradually did the ponds coalesce to form a lowly stream.

It was disconcerting because, so far as anyone could tell, it had never happened before. This silver thread of water had been winding down this valley before any men set eyes upon it; one might have supposed it would remain here, uninterrupted, even if men ceased to inhabit this land. Yet there in a mild, dry autumn the thread had snapped. 'Time must have a stop'—that may be a familiar proposition, in a poetic way; it was uneasy to find that the river, the local symbol of time's continuity, had anticipated it.

It was because of all the new land drainage, some say; or the boreholes up and down the country, which have lowered the water-table; or the general messing-about with nature; or even the weather, which is notoriously not what it was. At any rate it was agreed to be a regrettable phenomenon. People used to catch trout where the water had ceased to flow. There must have been a massacre among those humbler fish which still, in normal times, lurk in their hordes in the shallow water. I saw that those small ponds which marked the revival of the river after its arid half mile were seething with life; there might have been a heavy rainstorm beating upon the surface of the water, so agitated was it by the crowded refugees beneath, fighting for survival in their desperately reduced world. Casualties on the parched river-bed must have been fearful. It was a fishy combination of the Black Death and the hydrogen bomb and any other catastrophe you care to name, exterminating the population without quarter, drowning them in a terrible inundation of air.

I still saw the kingfisher patrolling the river-bed and I wondered how he had fared in these strange conditions. Perhaps life was easier with all his prey corralled in small ponds, instead of free to dart up and down the stream. Or perhaps the kingfisher also sensed, in some avian way, obscure dismay at the disruption of an immemorial part of the world of kingfishers. It was a cheerful day when the December rains had at last done their work, and the murmur of falling water was heard again from the sluice, and the river began to stir itself again among the fallen leaves which had usurped its place.

And now, in the aftermath of the rains, we are moving once again towards the halcyon days. The country is sinking into winter. One day of leaden skies followed another, with no movement in the moist air, only a noiseless drip from every hedge and tree. To be frank, this December ebbing-away of life can grow tedious. The spirits lift when (as happened last night) there comes a sudden and welcome change. The clouds disappeared, the moon shone hard and bright, and there was a bite of frost in the air. Today brilliance had replaced greyness. A glistening white rime transformed everything and there was a promising patch of blue overhead. The zestful freshness rekindled a proper affection for the best of winter days.

When I set off up the hill which separates us from the next valley, there were sheets of morning mist hanging above the fields, and at first the sun was only a golden glow above the horizon. By the time I reached the level ground on the watershed between the two valleys, the landscape was brilliantly lit, while in the valleys themselves intricate convolutions of low-lying mist slowly shifted and faded. The countryside seemed more populous than it had done. There was much crowing and whirring of pheasants in the wood, a flock of starlings wheeled against the sun, and a tractor that was ploughing the gleaming earth was escorted by a black and white cloud of rooks and gulls. A dense hedgerow had been invaded by a swarm of assorted small birds, who filled the air with chirrupings as they feasted on the berries.

It seemed strangely easy to walk up close to these congregations of birds. I gave a farmer a startled moment, too, when I

walked within a few feet of him, out in the open country, before
he saw me. I deduced that with the brilliant sun at my back, low
in the December sky, I was the next best thing to invisible. I put
this tactical advantage to the test when I came to the place where
the river emerges from a group of trees and winds across a
stretch of marsh. A snipe was down by the water and I was on
top of him before he took off in a hasty zig-zag over the reedy
clumps.

After standing still beside the river for a few moments I suddenly saw that I was not alone. A kingfisher was perched on a
willow branch which arched over the rippling water, a mere
arm's length away. He too had failed to see me against the
brilliant sun at my back. He stared down at the water with his
fierce little button eyes while I, trying not to betray my presence
by the faintest movement, regarded his improbably brilliant
plumage and his bright red legs. After a motionless few minutes
he made a dazzling dive into the water, like a small rocket
plunging downwards trailing red and blue and green. He
flapped comfortably back to his branch with a three-inch fish in
his beak. After banging the fish against the tree, and after some
unsuccessful attempts, he succeeded in swallowing this and
resumed his fixed stare at the water. A minute later he dived
again and captured another victim. Before five minutes had
passed he had caught and eaten three of these fish and he was
visibly fatter.

I suppose I moved, or else he caught sight of me in spite of
the blinding light behind me. Our eyes met for a fraction of a
second. Then, from his perch beside me, he launched himself
towards the distance with a final flash of colour over the water.

What could better have added lustre to this halcyon day than
this vision of the halcyon bird? The mist had gone, the sky was
uninterruptedly blue, the light was golden. The morning frost
had left only a delectable coolness in the air. The river flowed
past as if nothing in creation could ever interrupt its eternal,
tranquil course, and the water-weed swayed, gently and unceasingly, in the dark channel beside the bank.

It was even satisfying when this December perfection vanished
almost as quickly as the kingfisher had done; as satisfying as
putting the right frame around a painting. The sky filled up

with cloud and within an hour there was a damp mist over everything. By the time I reached home winter was showing an altogether different countenance. The mind turned to the pleasures of brightly burning logs behind closed curtains, with the owls calling in the wintry darkness. If I were condemned to live in the sweating monotony of the tropics, it would be the memory of just such a day which would most sharply stab me with the pangs of nostalgia.

EIGHTEEN

We went up to the wood looking for holly with berries, and it proved a more difficult search than would have seemed likely a couple of months ago, when every hedge offered a rich choice of fruits. The birds have been feasting since then. Every year, as Christmas approaches, we look at the hollies in a calculating spirit, noting the weight of the crop of berries, their probable accessibility to the gatherer of Christmas decorations, and the chances of their survival until Christmas Eve; and almost every year, we see plenty giving place to scarcity. In the end there is usually enough to go round, at least for those able to go out and look for it. The holly, a mysterious tree on several counts, has one useful peculiarity. Its berries are eaten eagerly by the birds, but in most winters a few of the trees seem to be out of favour, so that their berries are only nibbled at rather than devoured, or are even ignored altogether. It is these despised trees that we rely upon. As a gardener said to me once when gathering cherries, we have to be grateful for the birds' leavings.

Eventually we found enough today. There is never any temptation to be greedy, holly-boughs being the most awkward and uncomfortable of objects to carry; but even so, it was almost dark by the time we turned for home. The air was frosty and the sky clear. Plainly it was going to be one of those cold, static December nights when the owl's calls seem to echo in an empty world. As if to emphasise this, an owl materialised silently in the dim light overhead, an impressive, uneasy spectre beneath the trees, inspecting us at leisure before making a noiseless departure through a tangle of branches. A pigeon had crashed through the same trees in clattering confusion a few minutes earlier. The owl lifted itself upwards without a sound.

The valley passed from dusk to darkness almost as silently. At one place there was a subdued flapping overhead as the rooks settled themselves for the long night. A party of mallard, scarcely visible on their last flight of the day, crossed the sky with a soft swishing of the air. A blackbird, hidden in a dense hawthorn, suddenly panicked and plunged away into the shadows, trailing its shrill alarm call. But all the time a chilly stillness was spreading over the land. When we reached home the flickering firelight seen through a window was wonderfully inviting, as if a small overflow of domestic warmth had spilled out into the cold blackness of the lane. We carried the holly into the dark woodshed. After that, to go indoors, and to thaw numbed fingers before the leaping flames, and to feel the grateful comfort of the warm room, was a moment of delight: a primitive joy, one which men in any countryside gripped by winter have surely relished throughout time.

Walking down the hill I had thought of the many generations of village men who made their way homewards along that same path in winters past, chilled and weary perhaps after long labour in hard weather. Some poor devils would have had cold hearths awaiting them, no doubt; but the rest, as they looked down into the darkening valley, would feel a lifting of the spirits at the thought of their own fires burning companionably down in the village. I decided that only country people can know the full contentment of a fine fire on a winter night. It depends upon more than fuel and flames; it needs also the knowledge that a frozen world of hard earth and lonely hillside and owl-haunted darkness begins, like a black ocean pressing against a sea-wall, upon one's own threshold.

All such pleasures of comfort are only to be enjoyed to the full if the element of contrast be present. One must have been cold to appreciate warmth, one must be tired to understand the luxury of repose; and herein is one of the rewards of country life, in a time when civilised man exerts himself to eliminate all such satisfying contrasts from the daily routine. The countryman is still lucky enough to be cold and tired at times, and so to know the glow of pleasure that follows. A life without contrast is a deprivation of the spirit and the imagination; it is also a life robbed of those physical satisfactions which once carried a luxuriance of pleasure into the meanest existence.

There are limits beyond which I would not seek to pursue the point. The Victorians made something of a cult of discomfort, which now seems excessive. Today, for example, I found this in the diary of the Reverend Francis Kilvert, curate of Clyro in Radnor, which I consulted to find his account of his Christmas Day in 1870—and a cheerful account it was.

'As I lay awake praying in the early morning I thought I heard a sound of distant bells. It was an intense frost. I sat down in my bath upon a sheet of thick ice which broke in the middle into large pieces whilst sharp points and jagged edges stuck all round the sides of the tub like chevaux de frise, not particularly comforting to the naked thighs and loins, for the keen ice cut like broken glass. The ice water stung and scorched like fire. I had to collect the floating pieces of ice and pile them on a chair before I could use the sponge and then I had to thaw the sponge in my hands for it was a mass of ice.

'The morning was most brilliant . . .'

A hundred and more Christmases later, I admit to a certain respect for that formidable Victorian hardihood, but I shall not try to emulate it. Nevertheless, in this Christmas countryside it is easy to understand how our earlier ancestors came to think of the fire and the hearth as sacred objects. At this season even we, in our pampered century, respond to their appeal at a deep level that no central heating system, however comfortable or convenient, can reach. How much more potent the spell of the hearth in harsher times! The old men, I notice, still give their fires and their fuel some of that solemn respect which was their ancient due. I suppose that most of us, in the modern way, take these things for granted much of the time, grumbling perhaps at what old Charlie the gypsy woodman is charging for logs, but never doubting that there will be logs when we need them. The old gaffers treat the business more seriously, as they learned to do in the different world of their youth, when a man had to ensure by his own efforts that his necessities were provided.

One of the oldest of them is my neighbour, who will soon be ninety. I suspect that never a day passes, in summer heatwave or deep midwinter, without his giving some thought to his fuel supplies and if possible adding to his store—a log or two from a felled tree, or a dead branch hauled from the wood to be cut up at leisure. Through all the four seasons he finds time to work about his wood store like a serious little gnome, and his slow, patient use of axe and saw yields more impressive results than the brisker attack of many men a quarter of his age. He has several outbuildings stacked to the rafters with firewood, all of it cut to the perfect length, precisely arranged according to thickness, and dried there for years so that each piece burns unfalteringly when its day for the flames arrives. Sometimes he invites callers to 'come and have a look at the wood', no doubt enjoying the envy and admiration it invariably calls up; and although he will probably have to live to be a hundred to use up all the fuel he already has in his hoard, he is as diligent as ever about maintaining it. The task is central to the pattern of his life, it always has been and it will continue to be.

Our own fire burns serenely enough on this Christmas Eve. The sprigs of holly are going up, the sound of approaching carol-singers is heard down the lane, the village is given over to cheerful domestic stir. I remember that every year our old neighbour gives us, as a Christmas present, one of his finest logs, which appears on the doorstep, unannounced, during Christmas Eve. When I go to look for it, there it is, a seasoned length of apple-wood which will burn to perfection. I like to see in this graceful offering something that springs direct from the ancient

106

country traditions of the Yule log, centrepiece of the old festivities in manor house and cottage alike. When it blazes in the hearth tomorrow, I shall hope that we are not immeasurably distant in spirit from all the families who have enjoyed their Christmas firesides here, through an immense span of years.